SOYFOODS Cookery

Your Road To Better Health

Louise Hagler

with introduction by
Mark Messina Ph. D. & Virginia Messina M.P.H., R. D.

Book Publishing Company
Summertown, Tennessee

ISBN 1-5067-022-6

Cover Design: Louise Hagler, Beverly Lacy
Cover Photo: John Guider
Back Cover Photo: Anita Whipple
Food Stylist: Louise Hagler
Interior Design: Louise Hagler, Michael Cook, Jeffrey
   Clark
Art Work: Kim Trainer

Thanks to our neighbor Charles Jacobs for the fresh, green soybeans on the back cover

Pictured on the cover, clockwise from top center: Tofu Crème Parfait (page 138) with Creamy Tofu Topping (page 127), Soy "Coffee" (page 61), Miso-Ginger Dressing (page 66), Sweet-Sour Tempeh and Tofu Kebabs (page 98), Soy Protein-Tofu Burger (page 111) with Zippy Tofu Salad Dressing (page 76) and Soymilk.

Hagler, Louise.
   Soyfoods cookery : your road to better health / by Louise Hagler ;
   introduction by Mark Messina and Virginia Messina .
      P.   cm.
   Includes Index.
   ISBN 1-57067-022-6
      1. Vegetarian cookery. 2. Soyfoods I. Title.
   TX837.H23   1996
   641.6'5655--dc20   95-52962
                                                       CIP

Calculations for the nutritional analyses in this book are based on the average number of servings listed with the recipes and the average amount of an ingredient if a range is called for. Calculations are rounded up to the nearest gram. If two options for an ingredient are listed, the first one is used. Not included are fat used for frying, unless the amount is specified in the recipe, optional ingredients, or servings suggestions.

CONTENTS

FOREWORD

by Louise Hagler

Soyfoods have been the mainstay of my diet for over 25 years. My first experience with soyfoods was in the mid 1960s as a teenager dining in Seattle's Japanese restaurants. I was intrigued by the tofu that was served as a component in sukiyaki. At that time I had no idea what a large part of my life that quivering white curd, along with other soyfoods, would become.

Since 1971 I have been part of an intentional community in Tennessee called The Farm. We have experimented with all kinds of alternative ways of doing things over the years in search of a simple but graceful lifestyle that could be globally attainable. In the early days of the community, we created a healthful vegetarian diet based on the soybean. We viewed soyfoods as an ecological, economical, and versatile source of complete protein for feeding an overcrowded, hungry planet. As a group we worked together to make it work for us. We set about inventing recipes that were familiar to us but based on soyfoods. We shared our experiences and the fruits of our creations, supporting each other in the process. The result was a richly varied, tasty, healthful, and economical way to eat. This community co-operation also gave birth to two books, *The Farm Vegetarian Cookbook* and *Tofu Cookery,* Book Publishing Co. Summertown, TN.

Soybeans are abundantly nutritious, multi-faceted in use, and produce more usable protein per acre than any other food crop. This has a special significance in areas of the world where food and arable land are scarce. Soyfoods can be easily adapted to fit into most cuisines. Some of us have had the opportunity to introduce soyfoods into other parts of the world, where it has made a tremendous difference in the health and well-being of the people. I know hundreds of healthy adults, young people, and growing children raised on a soy-based diet who are living proof of the nutritional value of the soybean and a vegetarian diet.

Vegetarians or non-vegetarians can benefit from the remarkable properties of soyfoods. Beyond their nutritional value, soyfoods are being studied for their ability to treat and/or prevent disease. My sincere and grateful thanks goes to Mark and Virginia Messina for sharing their knowledge and expertise on the very special healthful qualities of soyfoods in the following introduction.

I am still cooking and experimenting with all kinds of these extraordinary foods. I have continued to develop recipes for a healthful array of tasty soyfood dishes to please both the palate and the pocketbook. Tofu, tempeh, soymilk, miso, textured vegetable protein, and other readily available soyfoods are culinary chameleons that can enhance your everyday meals in so many pleasing and easy ways. The recipes in this book present delicious, easy-to-prepare, familiar dishes incorporating soyfoods of all kinds. Add a little soy to your life and be on your road to better health!

INTRODUCTION

**By Mark Messina Ph.D. and
Virginia Messina M.P.H., R.D.**

Soyfoods have played a starring role in the cuisine of Asian countries for hundreds of years. Although they represent a somewhat new way of eating for Americans, they're being embraced with increasing enthusiasm. One survey showed that 26 million Americans include soyfoods in their diet. Chances are, those numbers will increase in the not too far future. Soyfoods are becoming big news as scientists accumulate more and more data on the relationship of these ancient foods to health.

Why all the interest in soyfoods? There are two reasons. First, healthful eating means a shift to a more plant-based diet. Soyfoods go a long way towards making this shift easier. They are rich in nutrients so they can help to round out a diet and make it more nutritious. And, given their versatility and ease of preparation, they make healthful menu planning a snap. In particular, the variety of soy products on the market, and the many ways in which these foods can step in to replace meat and dairy products in recipes, means that soyfoods fit right into healthier plant-based menus. Here are some of the ways that soyfoods can contribute to a more healthful eating pattern:

- Like all plant foods, soyfoods are free of cholesterol. They are also low in saturated fat. Replacing meat in your diet with dishes that include tofu, tempeh, and textured vegetable protein will reduce your intake of cholesterol and saturated fat and can lower your total fat consumption as well.
- Many soyfoods (particularly whole soybeans, tempeh, and textured vegetable protein) provide fiber. They contain both

soluble and insoluble fiber which are related to reduced risk for both heart disease and cancer. Most Americans eat far too little of this health-promoting carbohydrate. To boost fiber intake it is important to eat more plant foods in general.

- Soymilk, tofu, soy yogurt, soy ice cream (and recipes that include these foods) can stand in for dairy products in your diet. They lack the cholesterol and are low in the saturated fat that is found in both low-fat and full-fat dairy products. And they are free of lactose, the milk sugar that gives many people digestive problems when they consume dairy.
- Soyfoods are rich in nutrients including protein, calcium, iron, and B-vitamins.

SOYBEANS: A POWERHOUSE OF NUTRITION

Soybeans are legumes, a food group that includes beans, peas and lentils. As a group, these foods are rich in protein and fiber and low in fat. Soybeans are somewhat unique among legumes because they are exceptionally high in excellent quality protein, and they are also quite a bit higher in fat than other legumes. About 35% of the calories in soybeans come from protein, and about 40% of the calories come from fat.

The higher fat content of soybeans is a concern for some people. There are, however, an increasing number of reduced-fat soy products on the market, such as low-fat soymilk and low-fat tofu. Some soy products, like textured vegetable protein, are fat-free. There are also two advantages to the types of fat found in soyfoods. First, this fat is mostly unsaturated. Replacing meat, cheese, and whole and low-fat milk in the diet with soyfoods can help to lower your cholesterol. Second, soybeans contain a type of fatty acid that is essential in the diet and is relatively low in plant foods. It's called linolenic acid, which is one of the omega-3 fatty acids. Omega-3 fatty acids are linked to reduced cancer and heart disease.

Although scientists have long known that soybeans are high in protein, the actual quality of that protein has been undervalued. Protein quality is based on how well a protein is digested and on the specific pattern of amino acids (the building blocks of protein) in the food. In years past, proteins were evaluated by feeding them to young rats and mice and seeing how well they grew. Animals fed soybean protein didn't grow nearly as well as those fed animal protein. It is now recognized that this is because rodents have especially high needs for particular amino acids that are relatively low in soybeans. But humans don't have a high need for these particular amino acids. In fact, the pattern of amino acids in soybeans is very well suited to the physiologic needs of humans. Today, the old rodent-growth model for evaluating protein has been discarded. Using better methods now available, scientists have established that the quality of soy protein is equal to that of protein from animal foods.

Health-conscious people have known for decades that soyfoods are a fun and healthful addition to diets. But today, the excitement regarding these foods centers on some very special attributes of soybeans that have to do with much more than their nutrient content. Scientists are studying soybeans for their ability to prevent and/or treat several chronic diseases including cancer, heart disease, osteoporosis, kidney disease, and for their ability to relieve the symptoms of menopause.

SOY AND CANCER

During the past decade, hundreds of scientific papers have described some of the cancer fighting aspects of the soybean. These suggest that adding as little as one serving of soyfoods a day to your diet can help to reduce risk for cancer of the breast, colon, rectum, lung, prostate, and stomach and perhaps leukemia. Although the information is still speculative (that is, we can't say for certain that soy will reduce your cancer risk), there is enough information to justify adding soyfoods to the diet.

On the one hand, it isn't all that surprising that soyfoods might have this effect. Diet certainly impacts our risk for developing cancer. The National Cancer Institute estimates that one-third of all cancer deaths are due to poor diet, and some experts say that as much as one-half of all cancer is linked to diet. A cancer-defying diet is one that is rich in fruits and vegetables, low in fat, and high in fiber. In short, it's different from the way most Americans eat.

Soybeans: A Phytochemical Factory

Humans have known for many hundreds of years that plants contain powerful means for curing or preventing disease. Modern medicine continues to make good use of that knowledge and to build on it with scientific tests. Today, 25 percent of the drugs used in Western medicine come from plants.

In 1990, scientists from around the world gathered at a National Cancer Institute workshop to identify the parts of the soybean that might reduce cancer risk. They were able to name five types of compounds that show the potential to fight cancer (and agreed that there are probably several more). However, most of their attention was focused on one group of chemicals called *isoflavones*.

Isoflavones are part of a larger group of substances called *phytochemicals*. The phytochemicals are substances that have biological activity and, in many cases, demonstrated effects on health, but they aren't nutrients like vitamins and minerals. There are no specific nutritional diseases associated with the absence of phytochemicals in the diet. They aren't necessary to support life. However, they may be necessary to promote optimal health.

The prefix *phyto* refers to plants. So phytochemicals are plant chemicals. They aren't found in any animal foods. But most plants, including the ones we use for foods, are rich in a variety of phytochemicals. Isoflavones are a special group of phytochemicals though. For all practical purposes, you need to eat soyfoods to get them in your diet. No other food contains significant amounts of these chemicals.

Two of the isoflavones in soybeans have sparked the most interest among nutritionists. They are called *genistein* and *daidzein*. Of these, genistein is the one that shows the most potential to prevent cancer. In fact, the interest in genistein has exploded in the past few years. In 1985, there was one scientific study published on this isoflavone. In 1994, there were nearly 300 papers in scientific journals on genistein. Isoflavones are sometimes called phytoestrogens (meaning plant estrogens). And they are, in fact, quite similar in their chemical make-up to the human hormone estrogen but with some important differences, as we'll see.

High levels of estrogen in the blood raise the risk for breast cancer and for other hormone-linked cancers such as cancer of the ovaries, endometrium, and uterus. Breast cells have receptors that "recognize" estrogen and allow the estrogen to bind to the cells. Once estrogen enters the cell, it is believed to be involved in a series of reactions that raise the likelihood of cancer cells developing. So how would soyfoods (loaded with plant estrogens) reduce the risk for these cancers? The answer lies in the fact that there are subtle differences between plant estrogens and human estrogen. Because of some differences in the chemical structure of the isoflavones, they actually act only as very weak estrogens. Genistein, despite its similarity to human estrogen, has only about 1/10,000 the strength of human estrogen. However, plant estrogens still look similar enough to human estrogen to confuse the body.

The estrogen receptors on the breast "recognize" genistein and allow it to bind just as they do for human estrogen. But genistein's estrogen-like activity is so weak that it doesn't have any effect on the development of cancer. The cancer-protective effects of genistein are due to the fact that it blocks the more potent, cancer-producing human estrogen from entering breast cells. There are only so many estrogen receptor sites on breast tissue. The more space taken up by genistein, the less opportunity for human estrogen to make its way into the breast cells. It is like putting the wrong key in a lock. It looks like the right key (human estrogen) and it fits into the lock (estrogen receptors), but it won't open the door (or in this case, begin the cancer process).

For this reason, isoflavones are often called "anti-estrogens." Although they have estrogen-like activity, the fact that their activity is weak and they interfere with the activity of the more potent human estrogen means that the overall effect is just the opposite of what human estrogen produces.

One interesting observation about this anti-estrogen effect of genistein is that it appears to be similar to the way that *tamoxifen*, a leading drug used in the treatment of breast cancer, acts. Tamoxifen also acts as an anti-estrogen. In addition to being used for the treatment of breast cancer, tamoxifen (just like genistein) is being studied for a possible role in the prevention of breast cancer.

Genistein and Non-Hormone Cancers

Although the anti-estrogen effects of genistein have received much attention, soyfoods actually affect a variety of cancers (not just those related to estrogen). For example, hundreds of studies have found that when genistein is added to cancer cells growing in test tubes, the growth of these cells is stopped. This includes cells that respond to estrogen and those that don't. So it appears that genistein acts against cancer in a number of ways. This is because genistein inhibits the activity of "cancer enzymes."

Certain enzymes are much more active (as much as 20 times more active) in cancer cells than in healthy cells. These enzymes are involved in converting normal cells to cancer cells and are an integral part of the cancer process. Many conventional cancer

11

drugs work to stop the activity of these enzymes. And so does genistein. In this way, genistein may reduce risk for all types of cancer. The evidence that soy is able to lower risk of non-hormone–dependent cancers is at least as strong as the evidence for breast cancer.

Soy and Cancer Treatment

Although findings about the cancer protective effects of soy are still considered speculative by scientists, they are strong enough and intriguing enough to warrant interest in soy for treatment of cancer.

Tumor growth depends on the growth of new blood vessels which deliver oxygen and nutrients to the tumor cells. The tumor itself stimulates the growth of these blood vessels (a process called *angiogenesis*). One of the most promising approaches to treating cancer is to stop angiogenesis with drugs. In laboratory studies, genistein stops the process of tumor growth (although it takes quite a bit of genistein to have an effect). In fact, initial findings indicate it inhibits this process in humans who have a noncancerous condition that involves excessive blood vessel growth. Again, these effects have been seen in only a few studies and are still speculative. But genistein may work in other ways to stop the growth of existing tumors as well. Cancer cells can develop the ability to push cancer drugs out of the cell, rendering them ineffective. Studies show that genistein is effective against even these kinds of cancer cells. And, one study has shown that genistein enhances the effectiveness of cancer drugs against leukemia cells.

Isoflavones in the Diet

The only way to get isoflavones into your diet is to eat soyfoods. No other commonly consumed food contains significant amounts of this phytochemical. Just one serving of soyfoods a day (1 cup soymilk or ½ cup soybeans, tofu, tempeh, or textured vegetable protein) may be enough to reduce cancer risk.

Although most traditional soyfoods are rich in isoflavones, these compounds can be lost in food processing. For example, many commercial veggie burgers are made from soy protein concentrate which tends to be low in isoflavones. Some products, like soy cheese and soy ice cream, are often so low in soy that they don't contain much in the way of isoflavones. Foods that are reliably rich in isoflavones include whole soybeans, tofu, soymilk, tempeh, soy flour, and textured vegetable protein.

SOYFOODS AND HEART DISEASE

Soyfoods may provide a new way to lower cholesterol and therefore risk for heart disease. High blood cholesterol (along with smoking, obesity, high blood pressure, and sedentary lifestyle) is one of the biggest risk factors for heart attack. Eating a diet that lowers blood cholesterol can have a significant impact on risk. Experts say that for every one percent decrease in cholesterol levels, the risk for a heart attack goes down as much as three percent.

Saturated fat, which is found mostly in meat, dairy, and eggs along with a few plant products, raises blood cholesterol levels more than anything else in the diet. Dietary cholesterol also raises blood cholesterol levels, but to a much lesser degree. Some types of fiber can cause moderate reductions in blood cholesterol levels. Soybeans and soyfoods can fit into a heart-healthy diet because they are free of cholesterol, low in saturated fat, and some are rich in the type of fiber that helps to reduce blood cholesterol. So substituting soyfoods for animal foods in the diet is a good way to reduce heart disease risk. However, there may be a more important advantage to consuming soy. Soy protein directly lowers blood cholesterol levels.

Since 1967 (nearly 30 years ago) almost 40 studies on the effects of soy protein on cholesterol have been performed. Nearly all of these studies have demonstrated that soy lowers blood cholesterol levels. In fact, for the past 20 years, the National Health

Service in Italy has provided soy protein free of charge to physicians who treat patients with high blood cholesterol. A summary of the effects of soy protein on cholesterol was recently published in a leading medical journal. The authors concluded the following:

- Out of 38 studies on soy protein and cholesterol, 34 found that cholesterol drops when soy protein is added to the diet or replaces animal protein in the diet.
- Including soy protein in the diet produced an average decrease in cholesterol levels of 13%.
- Soy protein was most effective in people with very high cholesterol levels.
- Soy protein was effective even in people who were already following a 30% fat, American Heart Association diet. That is, soy protein produced further decreases in cholesterol levels after people had already lowered their cholesterol with a low-fat diet.
- Soy protein lowers LDL-cholesterol (the bad cholesterol) but does not affect HDL-cholesterol (the good cholesterol).

The 13% decrease in cholesterol that is typical with soy protein translates to as much as a 50% decrease in heart disease risk. In some people, particularly those with very high cholesterol, the results are more dramatic. And the fact that soy lowers only LDL-cholesterol is a considerable advantage since many cholesterol lowering programs also produce a drop in HDL cholesterol (a change that can actually raise heart disease risk).

One problem with this approach to lowering cholesterol is that it takes a fair amount of soy protein to produce a decrease in cholesterol. Most people would need at least 25 grams of soy protein a day which is close to three servings of soyfoods. Some people could need more soy protein than this. For those who want to try this approach to reduce cholesterol, one way is to use soy protein beverages that provide as much as 20 grams of protein per serving.

And of course, soy protein should always be used along with a low-fat, fiber-rich diet. Although organizations like the American Heart Association recommend that diets be no more than 30% fat, greater reductions in fat intake are actually much more effective.

Beyond Cholesterol

Although high cholesterol is a major risk factor for heart disease, nearly half of all heart disease occurs in people with average cholesterol levels Obviously there are a number of factors that can raise heart disease risk. One of these is cholesterol oxidation.

Oxidation refers to the reaction of certain molecules in the body with oxygen. Oxidation appears to play a role in a whole host of problems and is also part of the aging process. Only when cholesterol becomes oxidized can it damage artery walls and begin the buildup of the plaque that leads to artery blockage and heart disease. Preventing cholesterol oxidation may be just as important as decreasing blood cholesterol levels. It appears that soy not only lowers cholesterol but inhibits cholesterol oxidation. In a recent study, when heart disease patients ate soy every day for six months they had only 50% the amount of oxidized cholesterol in their blood stream compared to patients who didn't eat soy.

And finally, genistein may impact heart disease risk as well. Like aspirin, genistein seems to reduce blood clotting; blood clots are a critical factor leading to heart attacks. Genistein also interferes with the multiplication of cells that make up artery plaques. Although it takes a fair amount of soy to lower cholesterol levels, it may take just one serving a day to reduce blood clotting, plaque formation, and cholesterol oxidation.

SOYFOODS AND BONE HEALTH

The United States has one of the highest rates of osteoporosis in the world. Osteoporosis is a disease in which bones become thin, brittle, and easily broken. Good nutrition helps to keep bones healthy. For example, both calcium and vitamin D are crucial to bone health. But a great variety of factors affect bone health. Even where calcium intake is high, osteoporosis still occurs. Physical activity is one of the strongest determinants of bone health; weight bearing exercise keeps bones strong. Both sodium and protein might have a negative effect on bone health, because they increase the amount of calcium that is lost from the body. Soyfoods can contribute to bone strength in three ways.

Replacing animal foods in the diet with soyfoods may help to conserve body calcium. Some studies have shown that diets high in animal protein cause more calcium to be leached from bones and excreted in the urine or feces. In general, protein from beans, including that from soybeans, does not have this effect. In fact, one study found that nearly 50% more calcium was excreted when subjects consumed animal protein compared with the same amount of soy protein even though both diets contained the same amount of calcium. Since bones are normally very dynamic (constantly losing and regaining calcium) some loss of calcium from the body is normal. But anything that increases this loss could compromise bone health, since it becomes difficult to consume enough calcium to replace what is lost. The extent to which protein actually affects bone health isn't known for certain, but it is possible that this is one way that replacing soyfoods in your diet can help to keep bones strong.

Isoflavones in soyfoods may actually inhibit the breakdown of bones. One of the isoflavones in soybeans, daidzein, is actually very similar to the drug ipriflavone which is used throughout Europe and Asia to treat osteoporosis. In fact, ipriflavone becomes most effective only when it is metabolized. One of the products of its metabolism is daidzein itself. And a recent study found that the isoflavone genistein inhibited bone breakdown.

Finally, many soyfoods are naturally rich in calcium, and some are fortified with it. Tofu is often made using a calcium salt (this is often referred to as calcium-set tofu) which makes it a very calcium-rich food. Whole soybeans, textured vegetable protein, tempeh, and fortified soymilk are also good sources of calcium. Many people believe that calcium from plant foods is poorly absorbed compared with milk. Actually, this is true for only a few plant foods. For the most part, calcium from plants is well absorbed by the body, and the calcium from soyfoods is absorbed as well as that from milk.

SOYFOODS AND KIDNEY DISEASE

The kidneys are clusters of mini-filters that sift unwanted chemicals out of the blood and excrete them in the urine. Diet can impact the activity and health of the kidneys. For example, in healthy people, eating a high-protein diet can cause the kidneys to filter at a faster rate, a sign that the kidneys are working extra hard and being somewhat taxed. Over time, this can cause kidney damage in those who are susceptible to kidney disease.

In people who already have kidney disease, a high-protein diet can have the opposite, but still damaging, effect. It causes the kidneys to filter blood at a slower rate, a sign that the kidneys are weakening. For this reason, people with kidney disease are often advised to eat a low-protein diet. But it seems that the type of protein in the diet may be as important as the amount. Soy protein doesn't affect the kidneys in the same way that animal protein does. When patients eat soy protein in place of animal protein, (but still consume the same overall amount of protein) their kidney function improves. For this reason, some researchers have suggested that kidney disease patients replace some of the animal protein in their diet with soy protein. This is good news

17

for kidney patients since experimenting with soyfoods can be much easier than cutting back drastically on total protein intake.

Another advantage for kidney disease patients lies in the effects of soy on cholesterol levels and cholesterol oxidation. Kidney disease patients often have high blood levels of cholesterol and are at greatly increased risk for heart disease. These high cholesterol levels can also further damage the kidneys. By helping to lower cholesterol and prevent cholesterol oxidation, soy can help to preserve kidney function and lower heart disease risk.

MENOPAUSE

Symptoms that sometimes occur with menopause can include night sweats and hot flashes. These are due to a loss of temperature control that is related to a slowed production of estrogen. Estrogen replacement therapy is sometimes used to control these symptoms. However, there is some concern about the use of estrogen replacement since it is associated with an increased risk for breast cancer. Because of their weak estrogen-like effects, soybean isoflavones may be an alternative way to control menopause symptoms.

In Japan, where soyfoods are commonly consumed, women are only one-third as likely to report menopause symptoms as in the United States and Canada. In fact, there is no word in the Japanese language for "hot flashes." It may be that even with their very weak estrogen activity, isoflavones are potent enough to reduce menopause symptoms. In fact, in one study, when women were fed soy flour, they experienced about a 40% reduction in menopause symptoms.

Since estrogen helps to protect against both osteoporosis and heart disease, women are at greater risk for both of these problems after menopause. We've seen that soyfoods may be protective in both these cases. Based on this, it seems as though

18

consuming a serving of soyfoods every day may be an especially good idea for women who are going through menopause.

PERSPECTIVE ON SOYFOODS

Most of these potential benefits of soyfoods related to heart
disease, cancer, osteoporosis, kidney disease, and menopause
are being intensely investigated by researchers throughout the
world. Although some of the information we have now is speculative, much of it shows very solid relationships to diseases.
Within a few years, we should have an even better understand-
ing of the benefits of soy. In the meantime, there is no reason to
wait to add soyfoods to your diet. Their rich nutrient profile
means that they make a great addition to any diet. And, they may
offer health benefits to protect you and your family against a host
of chronic diseases.

Mark Messina, M.S. Ph.D. received a masters degree in nutrition from the University of Michigan in 1982 and a Ph.D. in nutrition from Michigan State University in 1987. His doctorate research involved the effects of cruciferous vegetables on colon cancer. From 1987 to 1992, Dr. Messina was program director in the Diet and Cancer Branch, National Cancer Institute, National Institutes of Health. His primary responsibility was to identify research needs in the area of a diet and cancer prevention and to make recommendations for government funding of research projects. In 1990, Dr. Messina organized a workshop on the role of soy in cancer prevention. As a result of this effort, the National Cancer Institute allocated three million dollars towards research on soybeans. From 1991-1992, Dr. Messina was also head of the National Cancer Institute's Designer Foods Program. This program focused on developing foods high in anti-carcinogenic phytochemicals for use in research. Since leaving the National Cancer Institute, Dr. Messina has devoted much of his time to the study of the health benefits of soyfoods. He writes extensively on this subject, and has given more than 100 presentations to both consumer and professional groups. He co-edits and writes a regular column for the **The Soy Connection,** a quarterly newsletter sent to the 70,000 members of the American Dietetic Association. In February of 1994, Dr. Messina organized and chaired "The First International Symposium on the Role of Soy in the Prevention and Treatment of Chronic Disease." Dr. Messina is organizing the second international symposium on this subject to be held September, 1996, in Brussels. He is the co-author, along with his wife, Virginia Messina, M.P.H., R.D., and Kenneth Setchell, Ph.D., of **The Simple Soybean and Your Health**.They are working together on two more books about plant-based diets, **The Vegetarian Way** and **The Dieticians Guide to Vegetarian Diets: Issues and Applications**.

Virginia Messina, M.P.H., R.D. is a registered dietitian with a masters in public health nutrition from the University of Michigan. She has taught nutrition at the university level, was a foods and nutrition specialist for the Michigan Cooperative Extension Service, and was director of nutrition services for George Washington University Ambulatory Medical Center. She was editor of the magazine **Guide to Healthy Eating** and is past editor of a newsletter for nutrition professionals **Issues in Vegetarian Dietetics**. Ms. Messina writes for a variety of publications including a regular column for vegetarian teens in the publication **How On Earth** and serves on Board of Advisors for **Veggie Life** magazine. She also writes regularly on plant food issues for the **Encyclopedia Britannica**. Ms. Messina is the co-author of **The Vegetarian No-Cholesterol Barbecue Book, The Vegetarian No-Cholesterol Family Style Cookbook, The Simple Soybean and Your Health, The Vegetarian Way,** and **The Dietitians Guide to Vegetarian Diets: Issues and Applications**.

BASIC SOYFOODS

Soybeans were first cultivated and consumed in China several thousand years ago. Their use spread throughout the Asian continent, and soyfoods became a central element in most Asian diets. Historically in that part of the world, soyfoods were believed to be a medicinal food, helpful in treating kidney diseases, beriberi, water retention, anemia, skin diseases, and other ailments. Buddhist monks, dedicated to vegetarian dietary beliefs, helped to promote and spread the use of soyfoods. Soyfoods arrived in the West with Asian immigrants but their use was contained within their communities until the mid-twentieth century. In North America, soybeans are mostly used for animal feed and manufacturing products such as plastics, paints, soap, inks, and oils. New interest in the use of soyfoods began in the late 1960s and has mushroomed in the 1990s.

The basic, most readily available soyfoods are described below. There are more new, convenient, easy-to-prepare soyfoods becoming available all the time. Be sure to check food labels on all foods to know exactly what you are getting.

Whole Soybeans are usually found dried. There are many varieties, including black soybeans. Store soybeans in a dry, air-tight container. One cup of dried soybeans will yield 2½ to 3 cups cooked beans. Soybeans must be thoroughly cooked to a very soft stage to be digestible. When properly cooked, soybeans should be soft enough to easily squash with your tongue on the roof of your mouth. The most efficient way of cooking whole soybeans is in a pressure cooker (page 54). Stove-top cooking for even 9 to 10 hours does not yield a truly soft bean. Whole soybeans can be sprouted or roasted for coffee (page 61) or snack nuts (page 64). Try Soybean Burritos (page 55).

Soybeans contain some sugars that are not easily digested and can cause gas or flatulence problems for some people. Soaking and blanching the beans before cooking can help solve this problem. Adding some kombu seaweed to the cooking water can to help as well (page 55). The offending sugars are also removed in the tofu making process, making tofu very easy to digest. The culturing process used in making tempeh helps to break down these sugars, as well.

Fresh Green Soybeans are a treat not to be missed. Still green and soft in their fuzzy green pods, look for them fresh or frozen in natural food stores or Asian markets. They keep frozen for several months. You might have to grow them yourself or find someone who does (page 57).

Soymilk can be used in almost any way dairy milk is used, but has the benefit of being lactose-free. Pour it on your hot or cold cereal, bake with it, or use it to make yogurt, gravy, ice cream, or pudding. Whip up a Soy Berry Smoothie (page 148) or Cocoa Banana Soy Shake (page 147). It can tend to curdle in your coffee, although an effective soy coffee creamer is available (page 30). Fresh soymilk is made by soaking dried soybeans, grinding them into a paste, then adding them to boiling water, cooking for about 20 minutes, and straining. Soymilk is available whole or low-fat, lite, flavored, and fortified with vitamins B, D, and E, calcium, and beta carotene. (Look for brands that are fortified with B12, essential for vegans.) Unflavored soymilk is best for cooking. Most soymilk is sold in aseptic packaging, which doesn't need refrigeration until it is opened. Once opened, it can keep refrigerated for 5 to 7 days. Look for it in supermarkets and natural food stores. Fresh soymilk is available in some natural food stores or Asian markets. Check the expiration date on the package.

Complete instructions for making soymilk at home can be found in *Tofu Cookery,* Book Publishing Co. Summertown, TN.

Okara (Soy Pulp) is the residue which remains after soymilk has been strained. It still has significant nutritional content, including the fiber of the bean. It can be incorporated into a number of tasty dishes. Try Okara Soysage (page 50) or Okara Macaroons (page 136).

Soymilk Powder is dried, processed soymilk that can be rehydrated and used as you would fresh soymilk. It is available in full-fat and low-fat varieties. Store soymilk powder in a dry, sealed container in the refrigerator or freezer. It is available in natural food stores and by mail order.

Soy Protein Concentrates are highly refined soy protein containing about 70% protein. Soy protein concentrates were developed as a lower cost alternative to soy protein isolates used in manufactured foods like baked goods, baby foods, and meat processing. The processing results in a bland flavor and a lower isoflavone content (page 13).

Soy Protein Isolates are highly refined soy protein. They contain about 90% protein and are a highly digestible source of amino acids. They are added to a wide variety of manufactured foods in small amounts to enhance texture, taste, and protein content. Soy protein isolates can be found in some breads, baked goods, breakfast cereals, pastas, infant and geriatric formulas, meat substitutes, desserts, soups, sauces, and snacks. They are available in health food stores as a food supplement.

Tofu is probably the most widely available soyfood and the most versatile. Also known as soybean curd, it is a soft, white, delicate, cheese-like food, made by curdling hot soymilk with a coagulant, then pressing it into a block. Mild in flavor, tofu takes on whatever flavor is added to it. Tofu is produced in silken, soft, medium, and firm textures and in regular, low-fat or lite varieties.

Low-fat and lite varieties can be substituted in recipes calling for regular tofu and will yield a dish with lower fat content. While about half the calories in regular tofu come from fat, its calorie content is very low. You would have to eat a great deal to get an appreciable amount of fat (½ lb. of tofu contains 10 grams of fat). Tofu is very low in saturated fat. Most of the fat it does contain actually helps lower the risk of heart disease and may help lower the risk of cancer (page 7).

Tofu is sold fresh, refrigerated, in bulk, water packed, or vacuum packed as well as in aseptic packaging that needs no refrigeration until it is opened. Look for tofu in supermarkets, natural food stores, and Asian markets. In supermarkets it is usually found in the produce section, although some stores have special dairy or deli sections for tofu.

When you bring fresh tofu home, it needs to be stored in the refrigerator under cold water. Rinse the tofu and change the water it is stored in everyday. Taken care of this way, tofu should keep for about one week in the refrigerator. If it turns pink or starts to smell sour, throw it out. Always check the expiration date when buying tofu.

Silken or soft pressed tofu is the best variety to use when the recipe calls for blending. It is softer and more delicate than regular tofu. Medium pressed tofu is best for mashing, crumbling, or slicing carefully. Firm pressed tofu is best for slicing or cubing, or when you want the tofu to hold its shape.

Serve tofu at any meal: for breakfast, scrambled like eggs in Scrambled Tofu (page 34) or as Eggless French Toast (page 43); for brunch or lunch as Tofu Migas (page 35) or an Eggless Tofu Salad (page 91); as an appetizing Creamy Cilantro Tofu Dip (page 70); for dinner as Almond Grilled Tofu (page 113); or for dessert as Tofu Tiramisu (page 124) or Tofu Crème Parfait (page 138).

Tofu is easy to digest and chew, which makes it a good protein source for the elderly and young children. Try blending it with fruit or vegetables. Slices or cubes of very fresh tofu with just a sprinkling of salt or soy sauce and nutritional yeast is one of the favorite foods of our young children (page 31).

If you don't or can't use your fresh tofu before its expiration date, wrap it in plastic or foil, and put it in the freezer. It becomes light brown in color and develops a chewy texture. It will keep frozen for several months. To use frozen tofu, thaw the tofu and carefully squeeze the water out of it. Cut or tear the thawed tofu into whatever shape you like. The tofu will absorb any flavoring you add to it. Try Thai Tofu in Peanut Sauce (page 119) or Honey Mustard Nuggets (page 116).

Tofu is also widely available grilled, deep fried, marinated, baked, and barbecued and ready to eat. If you want to try making these at home, see Oven Fried Tofu (page 114), or Barbecue Tofu (page 94). Complete instructions for making tofu at home can be found in *Tofu Cookery*.

Freeze-dried Tofu originated as a specialty created to preserve tofu. It is popular today with vegetarian hikers for a compact, light, high-protein food to carry in backpacks. To reconstitute freeze-dried tofu, soak it in cold water until it swells, carefully squeeze out the water, and add to soups or stews. Look for freeze-dried tofu that has a light, uniform color. The color of freeze-dried tofu darkens with age.

Tempeh is a cultured soyfood, usually made from soybeans or a mixture of soybeans and grains. Originally from Indonesia, this bean cake has a mild, nutty flavor with a hint of mushrooms and a distinctive texture. It contains the whole bean, so it is higher in fiber and lower in fat than soymilk or tofu. Tempeh also contains significant amounts of calcium, B-vitamins, and iron. It is usually found in the freezer section of natural or health food stores and Asian markets. It should be kept frozen until use and will keep for several months in the freezer. Although the culturing process helps to make the soybeans digestible, tempeh must be steamed for about 20 minutes before being eaten. Try Sweet-Sour Tempeh Kebabs (page 98), pictured on the cover, and Deviled Tempeh Spread (page 71).

In Indonesia, this traditional food is made at home. If you want to make your own tempeh at home, starter kits are available from The Tempeh Lab, P. O. Box 208, Summertown, TN 38483.

Textured Vegetable Protein is a quick-cooking meat substitute that is low in fat and calories and high in fiber, calcium, and potassium. It is made from low-fat soy flour which has been pressure cooked and compressed until the structure of the fibers change, then is shaped into pieces of different sizes and dried. It is manufactured in granular form, which resembles ground beef, and in chunks both large and small. It can be purchased flavored or unflavored. It is available in health and natural foods stores as well as by mail order. It will keep stored in a dry, tightly closed container for several months.

Textured vegetable protein is rehydrated by adding ⅞ cup boiling water to 1 cup of the dry product. Once it is rehydrated, it must be refrigerated and used within a few days. Textured vegetable protein can replace all or part of ground meat or meat chunks in a recipe to lower fat, increase fiber, and introduce the benefits of soyfoods. Try Taco or Burrito Filling (page 106), Quick Chili with Textured Vegetable Protein (page 105), or Soy Protein-Tofu Burgers (page 111), pictured on the cover.

Miso is a thick, rich, salty, fermented soybean paste used for flavoring or as a condiment. It is very concentrated; a little goes a long way. There are many varieties available which vary in color, texture, taste, and aroma, like fine wines from different provinces. Miso is low in fat and calories, contains essential amino acids, some vitamin B12, and minerals. It has a high sodium content. The traditional Japanese diet starts the day with a steaming bowl of miso soup. Try dissolving 1 tablespoon miso in a cup of hot water for a low-calorie, savory hot drink or soup base. Do not let it boil.

In Japan, miso is considered a medicinal food. It has been found to help prevent radiation sickness and neutralize the effects of environmental pollution on the body. Unpasturized miso contains enzymes and bacteria that aid digestion. Look for miso in natural food stores and Asian markets. It should be stored in the refrigerator and will keep for several months. Try Miso-Tofu Soup (page 79) or Miso Salad Dressing (page 67), pictured on the cover.

Soy Flour or Grits are made by grinding or cracking soybeans that have been toasted or heat-treated. Soy flour is available full-fat with all its natural oils or de-fatted with the oils removed. Soy flour or grits should be refrigerated or kept in the freezer to keep them from going rancid. It is a heavy flour and can be added to other flours in small amounts for baking. It adds moisture and texture to baked goods. Try replacing some of the wheat flour in a recipe with 1 to 4 tablespoons of soy flour per cup. Baked goods with soy flour added tend to brown more quickly in the oven. Look for soy flour, refrigerated or frozen, in natural food stores. Try Soy Waffles or Pancakes (page 44) or Multi-Grain Potato Soy Bread (page 48).

Yuba or Bean Curd Stick or Sheet is the skin that forms on the surface of soymilk as it is heated. Fresh yuba is considered a delicacy in Asia and is often used to make vegetarian "meats" in Buddhist vegetarian cuisine. It is available in the West mostly in the frozen or dried form. Look for it in Asian markets, or make your own by carefully lifting the skins off simmering soymilk. Reconstitute the dried variety by soaking in cold water until pliable or boiling for about 20 minutes. Try Scrambled Yuba (page 36) or Yuba Pastrami (page 101).

Natto is a pungent, fermented soyfood traditionally served with mustard and soy sauce. Originally soybeans were inoculated

27

and fermented in straw, but now the process is done under controlled conditions. You will probably have to go to an Asian market to find it. Its strong taste and aroma will cause many to pass it by, but if you are feeling adventuresome, give it a try. Look for fresh or frozen natto. It should form stretchy, slippery threads between the beans. Fresh natto must be refrigerated and will last only about a week.

Soy Sauce is used for flavoring. It contains high concentrations of sodium, and has limited nutritional value. *Shoyu* and *tamari* are traditional, natural soy sauces that are produced by fermentation. This process can last up to two years. Most commercial soy sauces are fermented from 3 to 6 months under controlled conditions. Shoyu is made from wheat, soybeans, water, aspergillus mold spores, and salt. Tamari is made from soybeans, water, aspergillus mold spores, and salt and has a higher amino acid content than shoyu. It was originally a by-product of making miso and used for seasoning and pickling. "Synthetic soy sauces" are generally concocted from hydrolyzed vegetable protein, hydrochloric acid, corn syrup, caramel coloring, salt, and water. Read the label to be sure what you are getting.

Soy Oil is a food grade, vegetable cooking oil extracted from soy beans. It is light in flavor and odor and has a high smoking point when used for frying. Most oil labeled "vegetable oil" in the United States is soy oil. It is 100% fat. It is high in polyunsaturated fat and very low in saturated fat. It contains linolenic acid, (an omega-3 fatty acid) and alpha-linolenic acid, (an omega-6 fatty acid), otherwise primarily found in fish oils. Soy oil is one of the few known vegetable sources of linolenic and alpha-linolenic acid. Omega-3 fatty acids are believed to help lower the risk of heart disease and help prevent cancer (page 7). Omega-6 fatty acids are believed to help lower cholesterol. Heat and hydrogenation reduce the content of omega-3 and omega-6 fatty acids in soy oil.

Soy Lecithin is a by-product of soy oil production. It comes in liquid and granular form. Lecithin may lower cholesterol, but it would take more than most people could eat in one day to be effective. It is used as an emulsifier in foods like ice cream, chocolate, and some peanut butter where water and oil are mixed. Try Mango Soy Frogurt (page 142) or Vanilla Soy Ice Cream (page 143). Look for lecithin in natural or health food stores.

CONVENIENCE SOYFOODS

For those times when you don't have time to cook, take advantage of the growing number of prepared soyfoods available. With new, tasty dishes appearing everyday, there is a wide variety to choose from in both supermarkets and natural foods stores. When possible, ask your retailer for samples to find what suits your taste. Always check the ingredients and nutrition facts on the package to know what you are buying.

For fresh, ready-to-eat foods, check the deli case in your natural or health food stores for fresh tofu salad, tofu dips and spreads, baked tofu, tofu lasagne or other pastas, tofu cheesecakes, and other local specialties.

Frozen Soyburgers, always a popular item, are quick to cook. There are many different brands available.

Frozen Tamales and Burritos only need heating to enjoy a southwestern treat.

Frozen Soy Hot Dogs or Wieners come in a wide variety of flavors and textures.

Frozen Fat-Free Soy Ground Meat Replacement comes packaged in a tube like frozen sausage and can be made into meatless balls, meat-less loaf, shepherd's pie, crumbled on pizza, or fried like sausage.

Frozen Soy Pizza is ready to bake in the oven.

Tempeh Burgers are available in several flavors.

Frozen Tofu Lasagne, Stuffed Shells, Manicotti, Tortellini, or Ravioli only need baking or boiling.

Frozen Soy Breakfast Links or "Sausages" or Tempeh "Bacon" are welcome additions to a stack of pancakes or waffles.

"Ground" Tofu is a flavored ground tofu product used to replace ground beef in recipes. Find it refrigerated with the tofu.

Meatless Chili Mixes only need to be heated with beans, tomatoes, and onion.

Meatless Burger Mixes need only water or tomato sauce mixed in before they can be baked, broiled, or fried.

Soy "Cheeses" can be used to replace dairy cheeses. Sliced, grated, and cream type cheeses, either with or without casein, can be found in the refrigerator case. Many different brands with varying textures and flavors are available.

Eggless Soy Mayonnaise made from tofu is a delicious, cholesterol-free spread.

Tofu Salad Dressings are cholesterol-free and ready to pour on your salad.

Soy Ice Creams come in a variety of flavors and textures.

Frozen Pot Pies come in individual servings or full size.

Frozen Pocket Breads are filled with various vegetables combined with tofu or textured vegetable protein.

Instant Miso Soup is a dried, powdered soup that is packaged in individual servings. Add hot water for a quick soup or drink.

Eggless Soy Cake, Quick Bread, Pancake, and Waffle Mixes need only liquid added to be ready to bake.

Liquid Soy Coffee Creamer is available ready to pour in your coffee or cream.

Smoked or Baked Tofu is available vacuum packed in the refrigerator section of your natural foods store or supermarket.

FEEDING BABIES AND
CHILDREN SOYFOODS

We have watched our children be born and grow up healthy and thriving on a soy-based, vegetarian diet. We have also watched malnourished babies and young children in Guatemala regain their health and prosper on this diet. Our children love to eat soyfoods.

If you are healthy and well nourished, breast milk is the best food for your baby for the first 6 to 8 months of life. You can try introducing soymilk, tofu, or soy yogurt to your baby at 7 to 8 months of age, slowly, a little bit at a time, watching to see how the baby tolerates it as you would any new food. Give plenty of water along with these soyfoods, as they are concentrated. Blend the tofu until smooth and creamy if the baby is not old enough to chew. You can try adding different vegetables or fruits to the blend as they are tolerated. Mashed or blended soybeans *without the skins* can be fed to most babies at 8 to 10 months old.

Some children can tolerate soymilk, soy yogurt, and tofu while they cannot tolerate the cooked whole soybeans. Usually, by the time they are 2½ years old, they will outgrow any intolerance.

By the time they are a year old and can chew well, try serving mashed soybeans in a soft tortilla or a soyburger on a soft bun. Our young children love to eat slices or sticks of very fresh tofu either plain or with a little salt or soy sauce and a sprinkle of nutritional yeast. Another favorite is very lightly fried slices of tofu with a sprinkle of soy sauce and nutritional yeast. Oven

31

Fried Tofu (page 114) is a popular finger food with both young and older children. Try blending tofu, peanut butter, and honey for a creamy spread for sandwiches.

Serve the Light High-Protein Soy Bread (page 47) or the Multi-Grain Potato Soy Bread (page 48) by the slice, in sandwiches, or as toast. Soy Biscuits (page 41) with Creamy Country Gravy (page 40) is one of our childrens' favorite breakfasts. Of course soy puddings, ice cream, cakes, and cookies are usually well received.

Young people generally aren't impressed by the healthfulness of foods; they want the taste and texture to please them. If you have older children with "tofu phobia," try serving the Barbecue Tofu (page 94), Quick Chili (page 105), Sloppy Joe (page 117) Soy Crèpes (page 42), Soy Pancakes or Waffles (page 44), or Tofu Tiramisu (page 124). Keep trying. With so many options, there is bound to be something they will like.

BREAKFAST
BRUNCH &
BREAD

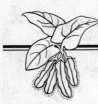

SCRAMBLED TOFU

Try Scrambled Tofu *in place of scrambled eggs for breakfast. Serve with toast or warm tortillas.*

½ cup onion, chopped
½ cup sweet bell pepper, chopped
1 clove garlic, minced
½ Tbsp. soy or olive oil
½ lb. tofu, crumbled
2 Tbsp. nutritional yeast, (opt.)
1 Tbsp. soy sauce

1. Sauté the onion, bell pepper, and garlic in the oil until soft. Add the tofu, nutritional yeast, and soy sauce, simmer until heated, and serve.

Per Serving: Calories: 143, Total Protein: 9 gm., Soy Protein: 9 gm., Fat: 8 gm., Carbohydrates: 7 gm., Calcium: 135 mg., Fiber 1 gm., Sodium: 513 mg.

MUSHROOM SCRAMBLED TOFU: Add 6 oz. sliced mushrooms of choice and ½ tsp. savory (opt.) to the sautéing onion, bell pepper, and garlic.

Per Serving: Calories: 165, Total Protein: 10 gm., Soy Protein: 9 gm., Fat: 8 gm., Carbohydrates: 11 gm., Calcium: 140 mg., Fiber 3 gm., Sodium: 516 mg.

TEX-MEX SCRAMBLED TOFU: Add 1 tsp. minced hot pepper to the sautéing onions, bell pepper, and garlic. Stir in 1 cup chopped tomatoes and ½ cup chopped cilantro with the tofu, yeast, and soy sauce.

Per Serving: Calories: 162, Total Protein: 10 gm., Soy Protein: 9 gm., Fat: 8 gm., Carbohydrates: 11 gm., Calcium: 145 mg., Fiber 3 gm., Sodium: 522 mg.

TOFU MIGAS

Tofu Migas *brings south-of-the-border flavors to any meal.*

¼ cup onion, chopped
1 small clove garlic, pressed
1 green chile or poblano chile, chopped
1 tsp. oil
¼ cup fresh cilantro, chopped
1 small tomato, chopped
4 corn tortillas, cut in sixths
½ lb. firm tofu, crumbled
½ tsp. salt

1. Stir-fry the onion, garlic, and chile in the oil until almost tender.

2. Add the rest of the ingredients, and stir-fry until all are thoroughly heated. Serve garnished with fresh cilantro and salsa on the side.

Per Serving: Calories: 267, Total Protein: 13 gm., Soy Protein: 8 gm., Fat: 9 gm., Carbohydrates: 33 gm., Calcium: 224 mg., Fiber 3 gm., Sodium: 551 mg.

SCRAMBLED YUBA

YIELD: 3 CUPS (4 SERVINGS)

Here is another alternative to breakfast eggs. Fresh or frozen yuba has the best taste (page 27).

6 oz. dried bean curd sticks,
   or 3-8oz. pkg. frozen bean curd sheet
½ cup onion, chopped,
   or 1 Tbsp. onion powder
2 cloves garlic,
   or ½ tsp. garlic powder
½ Tbsp. soy or olive oil
2 Tbsp. nutritional yeast
1 Tbsp. soy sauce
½ tsp. oregano
⅛ tsp. freshly ground black pepper

1. Boil the dried bean curd sticks in water for 20 minutes until soft, or thaw the frozen bean curd sheets.

2. Sauté the onions and garlic in the oil until transparent, add the rest of the ingredients, and heat through. Serve as you would scrambled eggs, with toast or warm tortillas.

Per Serving: Calories: 232, Total Protein: 21 gm., Soy Protein: 19 gm., Fat: 11 gm., Carbohydrates: 11 gm., Calcium: 98 mg., Fiber 0 gm., Sodium: 280 mg.

POTATO HASH WITH
SOY PROTEIN

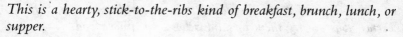

YIELD: 3 CUPS (3-4 SERVINGS)

This is a hearty, stick-to-the-ribs kind of breakfast, brunch, lunch, or supper.

6 Tbsp. boiling water
1 Tbsp. soy sauce
½ cup textured vegetable protein granules
¼ cup onion, chopped
¼ cup green pepper, chopped
1 clove garlic, minced
2 Tbsp. parsley or chives, minced
4 cups (1 lb.) potatoes, grated
¼ tsp. freshly ground black pepper
1 Tbsp. olive oil

1. Mix the boiling water and soy sauce, pour over the textured vegetable protein, and let stand for 10 minutes.

2. Mix all the ingredients together, except the olive oil.

3. Fry the hash in the olive oil in a non-stick pan until the potatoes are tender and browned, turning as needed. Serve hot with ketchup.

Per Serving: Calories: 194, Total Protein: 8 gm., Soy Protein: 6 gm., Fat: 4 gm., Carbohydrates: 31 gm., Calcium: 47 mg., Fiber 4 gm., Sodium: 298 mg.

TEMPEH STICKS

These can be served as an alternative to bacon, with pancakes, waffles, or French toast, or try them in sandwiches or as finger food.

8 oz. tempeh
3 Tbsp. water
1½ Tbsp. soy sauce
1 clove garlic, pressed
⅛ tsp. chipotle chile powder (opt.)
1½ Tbsp. olive oil

1. Steam the tempeh for 20 minutes, and cut into ¼"-½" sticks.

2. Mix together the water, soy sauce, garlic, and chipotle. Fry the tempeh sticks in 1 Tbsp. olive oil over medium heat until browned. Add ½ Tbsp. olive oil, and brown on the other side. Pour the liquid evenly over the sticks, and simmer until it is evaporated. Serve hot or cold.

Per 2 Sticks: Calories: 93, Total Protein: 7 gm., Soy Protein: 7 gm., Fat: 5 gm., Carbohydrates: 6 gm., Calcium: 32 mg., Fiber 2 gm., Sodium: 217 mg.

SAUSAGE FLAVORED SOY

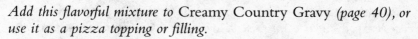

PROTEIN

YIELD: 1½ CUPS

Add this flavorful mixture to Creamy Country Gravy (page 40), or use it as a pizza topping or filling.

⅞ cup boiling water
1 Tbsp. soy sauce
1 cup granulated textured vegetable protein
1 tsp. onion powder
1 tsp. sage
½ tsp. thyme
¼ tsp. garlic powder
⅛ tsp. freshly ground black pepper
⅛ tsp. crushed red pepper
1 Tbsp. olive oil

1. Mix together the boiling water and soy sauce. Stir in the textured vegetable protein, cover, and let stand for about 10 minutes.

2. Fluff the hydrated textured vegetable protein into a bowl, and mix in all the flavorings. Cook in the olive oil over medium heat until browned.

Per ¼ Cup: Calories: 65, Total Protein: 7 gm., Soy Protein: 7 gm., Fat: 2 gm., Carbohydrates: 4 gm., Calcium: 34 mg., Fiber 1 gm., Sodium: 171 mg.

CREAMY COUNTRY
GRAVY

YIELD: ABOUT 4½ CUPS

This makes a thick, savory, creamy gravy for biscuits, potatoes, or whatever else you might want to serve with gravy. You can make a thinner gravy by adding a little more water. Use only unflavored soymilk to make this gravy. Using the microwave method eliminates the need for oil in the gravy.

½ cup unbleached white flour
2-4 Tbsp. nutritional yeast
2 Tbsp. canola or soy oil
4 cups soymilk,
   or 2 cups soymilk and 2 cups water or stock
1 Tbsp. soy sauce
3 tsp. poultry seasoning
2 tsp. onion powder
½ tsp. garlic powder
¼ tsp. freshly ground black pepper

1. ***Stovetop Method:*** Toast the flour and nutritional yeast in the oil until it starts to brown. Whip in the soymilk, leaving no lumps. Whip in the soy sauce, poultry seasoning, onion powder, garlic powder, and black pepper. Heat until it thickens and just starts to boil.

2. ***Microwave Method:*** In a 2-quart glass measuring cup, whip together all the ingredients (leaving out the oil if you like). Microwave on high for 4 minutes. Whip until smooth and microwave on high for 4 more minutes. Whip and serve.

Per ½ Cup: Calories: 94, Total Protein: 5 gm., Soy Protein: 3 gm., Fat: 5 gm., Carbohydrates: 8 gm., Calcium: 22 mg., Fiber 2 gm., Sodium: 128 mg.

QUICK SOY BISCUITS

YIELD: 6–8 BISCUITS

Soy flour adds extra protein and a sweet nut-like flavor to biscuits.

1½ cups unbleached white flour,
   or ¾ cup whole wheat flour and ¾ cup unbleached flour
½ cup soy flour
1 Tbsp. baking powder
½ tsp. salt (opt.)
¾ cup soymilk or soy yogurt
¼ cup canola or soy oil

1. Preheat the oven to 400°F.

2. Mix the dry ingredients together in a bowl, and make a well in the middle.

3. Mix the soymilk and oil together, pour into the dry ingredients, and mix with a fork just until the dough starts to form a ball.

4. Drop by spoonful onto a cookie sheet, or gently roll out and cut into biscuit shapes, and arrange on the cookie sheet. Bake for 10 to 12 minutes until golden brown.

Per Biscuit: Calories: 116, Total Protein: 4 gm., Soy Protein: 2 gm., Fat: 6 gm., Carbohydrates: 12 gm., Calcium: 34 mg., Fiber 1 gm., Sodium: 2 mg.

SOY CREPES

These crepes can be enjoyed by themselves or as a versatile base for either savory or sweet fillings and sauces. Try them spread with jelly or applesauce or filled with Scrambled Tofu *(page 34). Use them in place of noodles for manicotti.*

½ cup unbleached white flour
½ cup whole wheat pastry flour
¼ cup soy flour
¼ cup nutritional yeast (opt.)
½ tsp. baking powder
½ tsp. salt
3 cups soymilk

1. Mix the dry ingredients and make a well in the middle.

2. Pour in the soymilk and whip together. The batter should be very thin.

3. Heat a 10" non-stick crepe pan over moderate heat, and spray with non-stick spray. Pour in about ⅓ cup of the batter, tilting and moving the pan so that the batter covers the bottom of the pan with a thin coating. Cook until it is browned underneath and starts to pull away from the edge of the pan. Carefully flip it over and brown on the other side. Serve hot.

Per Crepe: Calories: 85, Total Protein: 5 gm., Soy Protein: 4 gm., Fat: 2 gm., Carbohydrates: 12 gm., Calcium: 35 mg., Fiber 2 gm., Sodium: 152 mg.

EGGLESS FRENCH TOAST

Serve this low-fat, cholesterol-free French toast with syrup, honey, or jelly and a side of Okara Soysage *(page 50) or* Tempeh Sticks *(page 38).*

1-10.5 oz. pkg. soft silken tofu
¼ cup soymilk or water
2 Tbsp. honey or maple syrup
2 Tbsp. nutritional yeast (opt.)
½ tsp. cinnamon (opt.)
½ tsp. salt
4-6 slices whole gain bread

1. Mix all the ingredients, except the bread, with an electric mixer, a whisk, or in a blender.

2. Dunk each slice of bread into the tofu mixture until coated. Brown on each side, either in a non-stick pan or a lightly oiled griddle. Serve hot.

Per Piece: Calories: 112, Total Protein: 5 gm., Soy Protein: 3 gm., Fat: 2 gm., Carbohydrates: 16 gm., Calcium: 15 mg., Fiber 3 gm., Sodium: 319 mg.

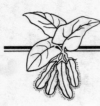

SOY WAFFLES OR
PANCAKES

YIELD: 6–4" WAFFLES OR 12–4" PANCAKES

Freeze what you don't eat, and reheat later in the toaster or microwave for a quick meal.

½ cup unbleached white flour
½ cup whole wheat pastry flour
½ cup cornmeal
½ cup soy flour
¼ cup wheat germ
1 Tbsp. baking powder
½ tsp. salt
2½ cups soymilk,
   or ¼ cup soymilk powder and 2½ cups water

1. Preheat a non-stick waffle iron or pancake griddle.

2. Mix all the dry ingredients together, and make a well in the middle.

3. Pour in the soymilk and whip until the dry ingredients are just moistened.

4. Oil the waffle iron or griddle, or spray with non-stick cooking spray. Pour the batter onto the preheated waffle iron or pancake griddle, and bake until golden brown. Use about ¼ cup batter per pancake or ⅓ cup per waffle. Flip the pancakes over when they start to bubble up, and brown the other side. Serve with syrup or jelly and Tempeh Sticks (page 38) or Okara Soysage (page 50).

Per Waffle: Calories: 201, Total Protein: 11 gm., Soy Protein: 6 gm., Fat: 4 gm., Carbohydrates: 30 gm., Calcium: 41 mg., Fiber 5 gm., Sodium: 191 mg.

OKARA-BRAN MUFFINS

These make a very moist, dense muffin, high in fiber and protein.

1½ cups whole wheat flour
1 cup oat or wheat bran
1½ tsp. baking soda
1½ cups soymilk
1 cup okara
½ cup sorghum, honey, or maple syrup
2 Tbsp. oil
½ cup raisins (opt.)

1. Preheat the oven to 400°F.

2. Mix together the flour, bran, and baking soda. In another bowl, mix together the soymilk, okara, sweetener, and oil. Pour the wet ingredients into the dry, and mix just until moistened. Fold in the raisins.

3. Pour into muffin tins and bake for about 20 minutes until they are browned and bounce back to a gentle touch of a finger.

Per Muffin: Calories: 159, Total Protein: 4 gm., Soy Protein: 1 gm., Fat: 4 gm., Carbohydrates: 27 gm., Calcium: 18 mg., Fiber 4 gm., Sodium: 7 mg.

EGGLESS BLUEBERRY
SOY MUFFINS
YIELD: 12 MUFFINS

Make these sweet, hearty muffins with either fresh or frozen blueberries. These muffins freeze well.

¾ cup unbleached white flour
¾ cup whole wheat pastry flour
½ cup soy flour
¼ cup wheat germ
3 tsp. baking powder
½ tsp. salt
1½ cups soymilk or Soy Yogurt (page 150)
½ cup honey
2 Tbsp. canola oil
1 tsp. vanilla
1 cup blueberries, fresh or frozen

1. Preheat the oven to 400°F.

2. Mix the dry ingredients together, and make a well in the middle.

3. Whip together the soymilk, honey, oil, and vanilla. Pour into the well in the dry ingredients, and stir just until blended. Fold in the blueberries, pour into oiled muffin tins, and bake for about 20 minutes until browned.

Per Muffin: Calories: 160, Total Protein: 5 gm., Soy Protein: 3 gm., Fat: 4 gm., Carbohydrates: 26 gm., Calcium: 25 mg., Fiber 3 gm., Sodium: 95 mg.

LIGHT, HIGH-PROTEIN
WHEAT-SOY BREAD
YIELD: 2 LOAVES OR 16 BUNS

Use this light bread with a sweet, nutty flavor to make sandwiches, toast, or just eat it by the slice.

3 cups soymilk
2 Tbsp. sweetener of choice
1 Tbsp. baking yeast
2 tsp. salt
4 cups unbleached white flour
2 cups soy flour
3-4 cups whole wheat flour

1. Scald the soymilk, dissolve the sweetener in it, and cool to lukewarm. Sprinkle the baking yeast over the top, and let stand until the yeast starts foaming.

2. Stir in the salt and flour, and beat until smooth. Beat in the soy flour until smooth. Add the whole wheat flour, and beat and knead until smooth. Cover and let rise until almost double in bulk.

3. Preheat the oven to 350°F.

4. Punch down the dough and form into 2 loaves or 16 buns. Let rise again until almost double in bulk. Bake the loaves for about 45 minutes or the buns for about 20 minutes. Brush the tops with soy oil.

Per Bun: Calories: 273, Total Protein: 13 gm., Soy Protein: 6 gm., Fat: 5 gm., Carbohydrates: 46 gm., Calcium: 83 mg., Fiber 6 gm., Sodium: 274 mg.

MULTI-GRAIN POTATO
SOY BREAD

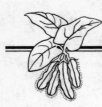

YIELD: 2 LOAVES OR 16 BUNS

Vary the flavor in this high-protein, multi-grain bread with whatever grains and flours you have on hand.

4 Tbsp. sweetener of choice
3 cups lukewarm potato cooking water
¼ cup soy oil
1 Tbsp. baking yeast
2 tsp. salt
3 cups unbleached white flour
½ cup rolled oats
½ cup quinoa
½ cup brown rice or barley flour
½ cup soy flour
3 cups whole wheat flour or spelt flour.
2 tsp. salt

1. Dissolve the sweetener in the potato water, and mix in the oil. Sprinkle the baking yeast over the top, and let stand until the yeast starts foaming.

2. Stir in the salt and unbleached flour, and beat until smooth. Beat in the rolled oats, quinoa, brown rice flour, and soy flour until smooth. Add the whole wheat flour, and beat and knead until smooth. Cover and let rise until almost double in bulk.

3. Preheat the oven to 350°F.

4. Punch down the dough and form into 2 loaves or 16 buns. Let rise again until almost double in bulk. Bake the loaves for about 45 minutes or the buns for about 20 minutes. Brush the tops with oil.

Per Bun: Calories: 260, Total Protein: 8 gm., Soy Protein: 1 gm., Fat: 5 gm., Carbohydrates: 45 gm., Calcium: 58 mg., Fiber 5 gm., Sodium: 270 mg.

OKARA-WHEAT BREAD

YIELD: 2 LOAVES OR 16 BUNS

Try this tasty, moist bread for an added measure of protein and fiber.

1 Tbsp. honey
2 cups warm water or soymilk
1 Tbsp. active dry yeast
4 cups whole wheat flour
3 cups okara
2 tsp. salt
¼ cup oil
4 cups unbleached white flour

1. Dissolve the honey in the warm water, and sprinkle the yeast over the top. Let rest for about 5 minutes until the yeast begins to foam.

2. Beat and knead in the whole wheat flour, okara, oil, and salt. Knead in the unbleached flour until the dough is smooth and evenly textured. Cover and let the dough rise until almost double in bulk.

3. Preheat the oven to 350°F.

4. Punch down the dough and shape into 2 loaves or 16 buns. Place in pans and let rise again until almost double in bulk. Bake for about 40 minutes for loaves or about 25 minutes for buns.

Per Bun: Calories: 252, Total Protein: 8 gm., Soy Protein: 1 gm., Fat: 4 gm., Carbohydrates: 45 gm., Calcium: 75 mg., Fiber 6 gm., Sodium: 271 mg.

OKARA SOYSAGE

YIELD: 24–30 SERVINGS

Serve Okara Soysage *with French toast, pancakes, or waffles. This recipe freezes well, so make a big batch to store in the freezer for later use. If you are going to freeze it, add the optional oil to help keep it from being crumbly after thawing. Try* Soy Oinkers in a Blanket *(page 51).*

4 cups okara
2 cups whole wheat flour
½ cup wheat germ
½ cup nutritional yeast
1½ cups soy milk
½ cup soy oil (opt.)
¼ cup soy sauce
2 Tbsp. garlic powder
1 Tbsp. oregano
2 tsp. salt
2 tsp. allspice
1 tsp. black pepper
1½ tsp. fennel seed
½-1 tsp. cayenne, or chipotle to taste
½ tsp. dry mustard

1. ***Oven Method:*** Preheat the oven to 350°F. Mix all the ingredients together. Pack into two oiled non-stick loaf pans or gently shape into 48 links or 30 patties, and arrange them on an oiled cookie sheet. Bake the loaves for about 1 hour. Bake the links or patties 15 to 20 minutes on one side then turn over and bake 15 to 20 minutes on the other side until browned.

2. ***Stovetop Method:*** Gently shape into links or patties, and brown in olive oil over moderate heat.

Per Serving: Calories: 65, Total Protein: 4 gm., Soy Protein: 1 gm., Fat: 1 gm., Carbohydrates: 10 gm., Calcium: 23 mg., Fiber 2 gm., Sodium: 314 mg.

SOY OINKERS IN A BLANKET

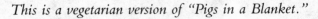

YIELD: 16 OINKERS

This is a vegetarian version of "Pigs in a Blanket."

16 link-shaped Okara Soysages (page 50)
Quick Soy Biscuit dough (page 41),
   or ½ recipe Okara-Wheat Bread dough (page 49)

1. Roll out the biscuit or bread dough, and cut out 16 rounds, triangles, or squares.

2. Wrap the dough around the Okara Soysage links, and bake on an oiled cookie sheet at 350°F until browned, about 12 minutes for the biscuit dough and 15 to 20 minutes for the bread dough. Serve hot with mustard and relish or sauerkraut.

Per Oinker (with biscuit): Calories: 125, Total Protein: 5 gm., Soy Protein: 2 gm., Fat: 5 gm., Carbohydrates: 15 gm., Calcium: 39 mg., Fiber 2 gm., Sodium: 186 mg.

Per Oinker (with bread): Calories: 164, Total Protein: 6 gm., Soy Protein: 1 gm., Fat: 3 gm., Carbohydrates: 28 gm., Calcium: 51 mg., Fiber 4 gm., Sodium: 220 mg.

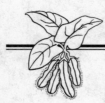

OKARA GRANOLA

YIELD: 5 CUPS (6 SERVINGS)

Here is a granola with the added fiber and protein of okara.

2 cups okara
3 cups rolled oats
⅓ cup sunflower seeds
2 Tbsp. sesame seeds
½ cup liquid sweetener of choice (honey, maple syrup, barley syrup, sorghum, or molasses)
½ tsp. vanilla (opt.)

1. Preheat the oven to 300°F.

2. Spread the okara out on a cookie sheet, and bake about 30 minutes until almost dry. Stir several times during baking. The length of time it takes to almost dry the okara will vary depending on how wet it was to start with.

3. Add the rolled oats to the pan, mix all together, and return to the oven for about 15 minutes, stirring at least once during baking.

4. Pour the okara and oats into a large bowl, and mix in the sunflower seeds, sesame seeds, sweetener, and vanilla. Spread the mixture back out on the cookie sheet, and bake another 10 to 15 minutes or until evenly browned, stirring frequently. Cool and store in a sealed container in the refrigerator.

Per Serving: Calories: 347, Total Protein: 11 gm., Soy Protein: 1 gm., Fat: 8 gm., Carbohydrates: 57 gm., Calcium: 94 mg., Fiber 7 gm., Sodium: 5 mg.

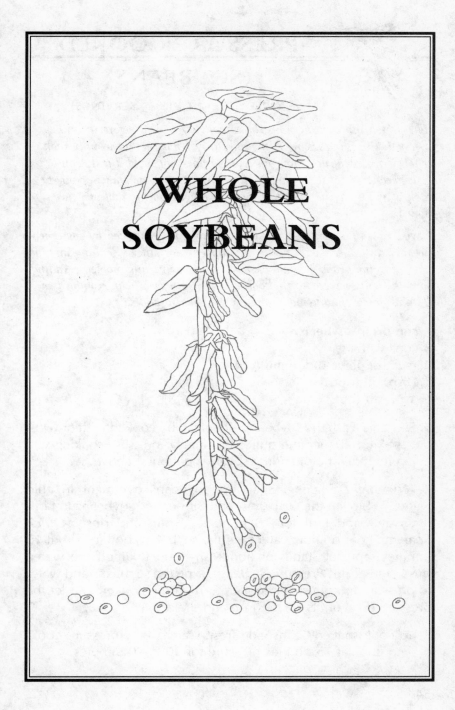

WHOLE
SOYBEANS

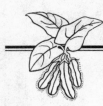

PRESSURE COOKED

SOYBEANS

YIELD: 2½–3 CUPS (5 SERVINGS)

The protein in soybeans must be thoroughly cooked before it can be digested. Pressure cooking is the only way I have found to fully cook whole dried soybeans. Stovetop cooking does not yield a truly soft bean, even after 9 to 10 hours of cooking. A soybean that is properly cooked will easily be squashed by your tongue on the roof of your mouth.

Soybeans contain some sugars that are not easily digested by some people and can cause gas or flatulence problems for others. Soaking and/or blanching the beans before cooking can help solve this problem. Adding some kombu seaweed to the cooking water can also help. Kombu is a natural flavor enhancer, eliminating the need to add salt.

1 cup dried soybeans
3 cups water
2" square piece of kombu (opt.)
1 Tbsp. oil (opt.)
½ tsp. salt (opt.)

1. Sort and wash the soybeans. They can be cooked with or without soaking. Blanching, quick soaking, or pressure soaking will help eliminate the offending sugars mentioned above.

2. ***Overnight Soaking:*** Soak the soybeans overnight in cold water. To blanch the soybeans, add the soaked soybeans to boiling water and boil for 10 minutes. Drain and rinse. ***Quick Soaking:*** Pour boiling water over the soybeans, boil for about 10 minutes, and let stand for about an hour. Pour off the water, rinse, and drain. ***Pressure Soaking:*** Bring the soybeans and water to pressure in a pressure cooker, turn off the cooker, and let the pressure drop on its own. Rinse and drain.

3. To cook soaked beans, add fresh water to the pressure cooker, and cook at 15 pounds pressure for 30 to 40 minutes.

4. Cook unsoaked soybeans at 15 lbs. pressure for 45 to 75 minutes. The average cooking time will be about 1 hour, but it will vary depending on the variety, age, and dryness of the beans.

5. The skins of the beans may tend to come loose and clog the pressure cooker vent. If the vent becomes clogged, bring the pressure all the way down, remove the lid, clean out the vent pipe, and skim off any loose bean skins that are floating on top. Reclose the pot, bring to pressure again, and continue cooking. Never leave your pressure cooker unattended.

Per Serving: Calories: 149, Total Protein: 12 gm., Soy Protein: 12 gm., Fat: 7 gm., Carbohydrates: 9 gm., Calcium: 88 mg., Fiber 4 gm., Sodium: 1 mg.

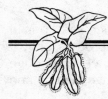

SOYBEAN BURRITOS

YIELD: 8 BURRITOS

Use wheat or corn tortillas or try Wheat-Soy Tortillas, and add chopped tomatoes and jalapeños or your favorite salsa. Sprinkle on nutritional yeast for an additional cheese-like flavor.

Pressure Cooked Soybeans (page 54)
wheat or corn tortillas or prepared Wheat-Soy Tortillas
   (page 56)
your favorite salsa
tomatoes, chopped
hot peppers, chopped (to taste)
lettuce, chopped
fresh cilantro, chopped
nutritional yeast

1. Fill the tortillas with the beans and fixings of choice.

Per Tortilla (using ⅓ cup for all ingredients): Calories: 223, Total Protein: 13 gm., Soy Protein: 8 gm., Fat: 5 gm., Carbohydrates: 31 gm., Calcium: 102 mg., Fiber 6 gm., Sodium: 216 mg.

WHEAT-SOY TORTILLAS

Yield: eight 10" tortillas

The best tasting tortilla is a freshly made one. A food processor or electric mixer with dough hook makes this much easier, although it can be done by hand.

1 cup unbleached white flour
⅔ cup whole wheat flour
⅓ cup soy flour
¼ tsp. salt
¾ cup warm water

1. Mix the flours and salt together in a food processor. Pour in the water while the processor is running, and process until it forms a ball and cleans the sides of the work bowl. The dough should not be sticky but soft and workable. Remove the ball and let it rest for a few minutes.

2. Form the dough into 8 balls about 1½" in diameter. They should roll out easily with little or no flour. Roll them very thin, less than ¹⁄₁₆" if you can do it.

3. Cook the tortillas on a hot, dry griddle. They will bubble up on the top side and brown on the underside of the bubbles when they are ready to be flipped over. The flip side cooks the same way. It takes only about 10 to 15 seconds on a truly hot griddle for each side. These tortillas are at their best served fresh off the griddle, but they can be stacked inside a moist cloth and reheated later.

Per Tortilla: Calories: 100, Total Protein: 3 gm., Soy Protein: 0 gm., Fat: 0 gm., Carbohydrates: 21 gm., Calcium: 28 mg., Fiber 2 gm., Sodium: 68 mg.

GREEN SOYBEANS IN
THE POD

YIELD: ABOUT 2 CUPS

These are a special snack treat in parts of Asia, served as an appetizer, an accompaniment to sake or beer, or a lunch box treat for children. The beans are harvested in the pod when they are almost mature but are still green and have not dried out. If you have garden space, they are easy to grow during the warm season. Green soybeans can sometimes be found in Asian or natural foods stores.

1 lb. green soybeans in the pod
2 cups water
½ tsp salt

1. Wash and steam or boil the soybeans in their pods for about 15 to 20 minutes or until crisp-tender. Serve in the pod but remove from the pod before eating.

VARIATION: Remove the soybeans from the pods, and steam or boil for about 15 to 20 minutes until crisp-tender. Serve as you would green peas.

Per ¼ Cup: Calories: 80, Total Protein: 7 gm., Soy Protein: 7 gm., Fat: 2 gm., Carbohydrates: 6 gm., Calcium: 84 mg., Fiber 1 gm., Sodium: 135 mg.

BAKED SOYBEANS

YIELD: 4 CUPS (6 SERVINGS)

This is a delicious way to serve leftover beans.

1 medium onion, chopped
1 small green pepper, chopped
2 cloves garlic, minced
½ Tbsp. soy or olive oil
3 cups Pressure Cooked Soybeans (page 54)
¼ cup sorghum molasses
¼ cup ketchup,
   or 4 Tbsp. tomato paste
1 tsp. salt
½ tsp. dry mustard

1. Preheat the oven to 350°F.

2. Sauté the onion, green pepper, and garlic in the oil. Mix all the ingredients together in a 1½-quart casserole dish, and bake uncovered for about 45 minutes. (If you don't have time for baking, heat thoroughly on the stovetop or in the microwave.)

Per Serving: Calories: 229, Total Protein: 13 gm., Soy Protein: 12 gm., Fat: 8 gm., Carbohydrates: 26 gm., Calcium: 116 mg., Fiber 4 gm., Sodium: 480 mg.

VARIATION: Add 2 soy "hot dogs" cut in chunks to the casserole mixture before baking.

Per Serving: Calories: 252, Total Protein: 15 gm., Soy Protein: 15 gm., Fat: 8 gm., Carbohydrates: 27 gm., Calcium: 116 mg., Fiber 4 gm., Sodium: 480 mg.

BARBECUE SOYBEANS

Add your favorite barbecue sauce to leftover pressure cooked soybeans, heat, and serve.

1½ cups your favorite barbecue sauce or the sauce below

For the Barbecue Sauce:
1-4 oz. can tomato paste
1 cup water
⅓ cup brown sugar
¼ cup salad mustard
1 Tbsp. onion powder
½ tsp. garlic powder
½ tsp. allspice
**½ tsp. cracked red pepper,
   or chipotle to taste**
½ tsp. salt

3 cups Pressure Cooked Soybeans (page 54)

2 Tbsp. vinegar

1. Mix all the ingredients, except the beans and the vinegar. Heat and bring to a boil. Reduce the heat to a simmer for 10 minutes stir in the beans and vinegar, and simmer until heated through.

Per Serving: Calories: 212, Total Protein: 13 gm., Soy Protein: 12 gm., Fat: 9 gm., Carbohydrates: 19 gm., Calcium: 103 mg., Fiber 4 gm., Sodium: 474 mg.

SOY BURGERS

Use your leftover cooked soybeans to make these burgers or Soy Non-Meat Balls (see variation below). Serve Soy Burgers on toasted buns with mustard, lettuce, and tomato. Soy Non-Meat Balls are a great accompaniment to pasta. This recipe is adapted from Lighten Up!— With Louise Hagler.

2 cups Pressure Cooked Soybeans (page 54)
½ cup oatmeal, uncooked or whole wheat flour
½ cup oat bran or wheat germ
½ cup onion, finely chopped, or 2 tsp. onion powder
1 clove garlic, minced, or ½ tsp. garlic powder
2 Tbsp. tomato paste or ketchup
1 tsp. salt
½ tsp. oregano
½ tsp. basil

1. Mash the cooked soy beans with a potato masher, or chop in a food processor.

2. Stir the mashed beans into the rest of the ingredients. Mix well and divide into 8 balls. Flatten each ball to about ½" thick or less. Fry on a non-stick surface sprayed with non-stick spray. Cook until browned on both sides.

Per Burger: Calories: 130, Total Protein: 9 gm., Soy Protein: 6 gm., Fat: 5 gm., Carbohydrates: 12 gm., Calcium: 53 mg., Fiber 4 gm., Sodium: 270 mg.

SOY NON-MEAT BALLS: Preheat the oven to 350°F. Form the burger mix into 24 balls. Spray a 9" x 13" pan with non-stick spray, or spread with 1 Tbsp. oil. Arrange the balls evenly in the pan, and bake for 30 to 40 minutes, rolling the balls every 10 minutes to brown on all sides.

Per Ball: Calories: 43, Total Protein: 3 gm., Soy Protein: 2 gm., Fat: 2 gm., Carbohydrates: 4 gm., Calcium: 18 mg., Fiber 1 gm., Sodium: 90 mg.

SOY "COFFEE"

YIELD: ¾ CUP GROUND OR 6–12 CUPS SOY COFFEE

Try soy "coffee" for a non-caffeinated brew any time of day. This recipe is adapted from The New Farm Vegetarian Cookbook.

1 cup soybeans

1. Soak the soybeans overnight or use the pressure cooker "quick soak" method (page 54).

2. Preheat the oven to 300°F.

3. Spread the soaked soybeans out on a cookie sheet, one layer deep. Bake in the oven until they are a dark golden brown, but not burned. This takes about 4 hours. Grind in a coffee grinder, while still hot if possible, and brew as you would coffee. Use 1 or 2 scant tablespoon of the ground beans per cup of water. You can also simmer it gently for about 5 minutes. Do not boil or it will be bitter.

Per Cup: Calories: 19, Total Protein: 2 gm., Soy Protein: 2 gm., Fat: 1 gm., Carbohydrates: 1 gm., Calcium: 11 mg., Fiber 0 gm., Sodium: 0 mg.

SOYBEAN SPROUTS

Crunchy, nutritious, and tasty, soy sprouts are easy to make at home and are sometimes available in Oriental or natural foods stores. Soybeans take anywhere from 5 to 10 days to sprout. These directions are adapted from The New Farm Vegetarian Cookbook. *For the best prices, purchase soybeans in bulk quantities from a food co-op. Make sure the soybeans have not been treated with mercury or other chemicals.*

Materials:
dry soybeans (about ¼ cup dry soybeans will fill a quart jar with sprouts)
water
container to grow the sprouts in—a glass jar with nylon or cheesecloth stretched across the top and secured with a rubber band; or a tray or cake pan, preferably glass or anything rustproof
colander for rinsing sprouting soybeans.

Basic Steps:

1. Rinse your soybeans well, about 3-4 times, to remove bacteria and dust.

2. Soak the soybeans overnight in lukewarm to cool water to germinate them. If you are spouting in a jar, soak them in the same jar.

3. Stretch some nylon or cheesecloth over the top of the jar and secure it with a ring or rubber band.

4. Drain by tilting the jar over a sink. If sprouting on a tray, drain the soybeans thoroughly in a colander, and spread them on the tray.

5. Sprout the soybeans in a warm, dark place. Spread the soy-

beans no more than 2 thick for proper growth. If you're using a jar, turn it sideways and shake the soybeans so they line the sides of the jar. If you're using a tray, line the bottom with a damp cloth, spread the soybeans, and cover with a cheesecloth.

6. Water the sprouting soybeans whenever they look dry (usually 2-3 times a day). A spay-mister is a good device to use for watering, especially when growing them on a tray. Soybeans sprouted in a jar can be rinsed under tap water, but they should be thoroughly drained.

Full grown soybean sprouts should be 1½" to 2½" long. Sprouts that are grown in the dark will be yellow. If the fully grown sprouts are placed in indirect sunlight for a few hours, they will develop chlorophyll and turn green. Before serving, submerge the sprouts in cold water, and agitate slightly. Most of the bean hulls will float to the top where they can be removed. Drain and serve or store in an airtight container or plastic bag in the refrigerator. They will keep refrigerated for a few days.

Per ½ Cup: Calories: 45, Total Protein: 4 gm., Soy Protein: 4 gm., Fat: 1 gm., Carbohydrates: 4 gm., Calcium: 24 mg., Fiber 1 gm., Sodium: 5 mg.

SOY NUTS

YIELD: 3 CUPS

Use the oven method for a lower fat snack. This recipe is adapted from The New Farm Vegetarian Cookbook.

1 cup soybeans

1. Soak the soybeans overnight or put them in a pressure cooker with sufficient water and 1 Tbsp. oil. Bring to full pressure and immediately remove from heat, allowing the beans to come down from pressure slowly. (Beans must be well soaked or partially cooked first, or they will be indigestible.) Drain well in a colander or strainer.

2. **Deep Fry Method:** Heat 3 cups soy oil to 400°F, and carefully add 1 cup soaked soybeans. Fry on full flame for about 7 minutes or until golden brown. Remove the beans and drain on absorbent paper. Salt to taste. Make sure the temperature of the oil is up to 400°F at the start of each batch. **Oven Roasting Method:** Place the beans on an oiled cookie sheet, one bean deep, and bake in a 350°F oven, turning occasionally, until golden brown, about 30-45 minutes.

Store soy nuts in an airtight container to keep crisp, and serve as high-protein snacks.

Per ¼ Cup (oven roasted): Calories: 50, Total Protein: 4 gm., Soy Protein: 4 gm., Fat: 2 gm., Carbohydrates: 3 gm., Calcium: 29 mg., Fiber 1 gm., Sodium: 0 mg.

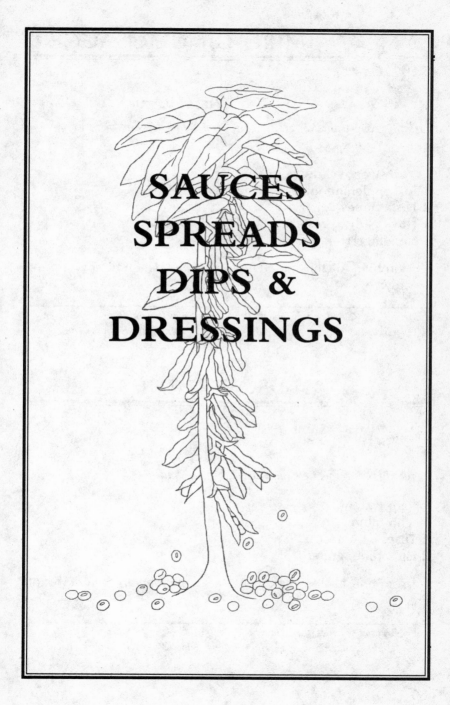

SAUCES
SPREADS
DIPS &
DRESSINGS

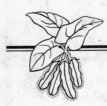

MISO-GINGER SAUCE

YIELD: ½ CUP

Use this easy-to-make, zippy sauce as a salad dressing or sauce for steamed vegetables.

⅓ cup sweet yellow miso
1½ Tbsp. lemon juice or rice vinegar
2 Tbsp. honey
1 clove garlic, pressed
1 tsp. gingerroot, grated

1. Combine all the ingredients in a blender until smooth and creamy.

Per 2 Tbsp.: Calories: 82, Total Protein: 2 gm., Soy Protein: 2 gm., Fat: 1 gm., Carbohydrates: 15 gm., Calcium: 17 mg., Fiber 1 gm., Sodium: 1 mg.

MISO-TAHINI SAUCE

YIELD: ½ CUP

Serve this sauce over steamed vegetables or grains.

¼ cup water
¼ cup tahini
1 Tbsp. dark miso
2 tsp. onion, grated

1. Combine all the ingredients in a blender until smooth and creamy.

Per 2 Tbsp.: Calories: 95, Total Protein: 3 gm., Soy Protein: 0 gm., Fat: 7 gm., Carbohydrates: 5 gm., Calcium: 66 mg., Fiber 2 gm., Sodium: 11 mg.

MISO SALAD DRESSING
OR SAUCE

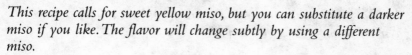

YIELD: 1 CUP

This recipe calls for sweet yellow miso, but you can substitute a darker miso if you like. The flavor will change subtly by using a different miso.

1 Tbsp. sesame oil
6 Tbsp. sweet yellow miso
2 Tbsp. rice vinegar
1 Tbsp. honey
2 tsp. onion, grated,
   or 1 tsp. onion powder
6 Tbsp. water

1. Combine all the ingredients in a blender until smooth and creamy.

2. To serve hot; heat, but do not boil. Serve over steamed vegetables, grains, or tofu.

Per 2 Tbsp.: Calories: 50, Total Protein: 1 gm., Soy Protein: 1 gm., Fat: 2 gm., Carbohydrates: 6 gm., Calcium: 9 mg., Fiber 1 gm., Sodium: 0 mg.

CREAMY MUSHROOM
SAUCE

YIELD: 3 CUPS (3–4 SERVINGS)

This is a perfect sauce for pasta. Round out the meal with steamed green beans and a crisp green salad.

1 lb. mushrooms, sliced
2 Tbsp. soy or olive oil
¼ cup unbleached white flour
2 Tbsp. nutritional yeast
3 cups soymilk
1 Tbsp. chives
1 Tbsp. soy sauce
2 tsp. onion powder
½ tsp. garlic powder
⅛ tsp. freshly ground black pepper

1. Sauté the mushrooms in 1 Tbsp.oil.

2. Remove the mushrooms from the pan, and add 1 Tbsp. oil, the flour, and nutritional yeast. Whip these together and let bubble over low heat for about 1 minute. Whip in the soymilk, chives, soy sauce, onion powder, garlic powder, and black pepper. Continue stirring with the whip until smooth and thick. Stir in the sautéed mushrooms, and serve.

Per Serving: Calories: 216, Total Protein: 11 gm., Soy Protein: 7 gm., Fat: 12 gm., Carbohydrates: 17 gm., Calcium: 41 mg., Fiber 5 gm., Sodium: 206 mg.

MISO-TOFU SPREAD

Yield: 1 cup

Serve this as a creamy spread for crackers and bread or as a dip for vegetables or chips.

1 clove garlic
½ lb. tofu
3 Tbsp. sweet rice miso
3 Tbsp. rice vinegar
2 tsp. onion powder

1. Chop the garlic in a food processor.

2. Add the rest of ingredients, and blend until smooth. Refrigerate for a few hours or overnight for flavors to blend.

Per 2 Tbsp.: Calories: 37, Total Protein: 3 gm., Soy Protein: 3 gm., Fat: 1 gm., Carbohydrates: 3 gm., Calcium: 35 mg., Fiber 0 gm., Sodium: 2 mg.

CREAMY CILANTRO
TOFU

Yield: 1¼ cups

Serve this in place of sour cream for any Mexican entrée or as an appetizer with chips or raw vegetables.

1 large clove garlic
1 small jalapeño (opt.),
   or ⅛ tsp. dried hot pepper
1 cup fresh cilantro leaves
1-10.5 oz. pkg. silken tofu,
   or ½ lb regular tofu + 6 Tbsp. water
1 Tbsp. lime juice
½ tsp. salt

1. Chop the garlic in a food processor, add the jalapeño, chop, add the cilantro leaves and chop. Remove from the food processor, and set aside.

2. Add the tofu, lime juice, and salt to the processor, and process until smooth and creamy.

3. Fold in the garlic, cilantro, and jalapeño. Serve chilled as a dip or condiment with Mexican food.

Creamy Cumin Tofu: Substitute 1 tsp. cumin powder for the cilantro.

Per 2 Tbsp.: Calories: 14, Total Protein: 2 gm., Soy Protein: 2 gm., Fat: 0 gm., Carbohydrates: 1 gm., Calcium: 3 mg., Fiber 0 gm., Sodium: 160 mg.

DEVILED TEMPEH
SPREAD

YIELD: 1½ CUPS

Spread this on crackers for a snack or in a sandwich with all the fixings for a meal.

8 oz. tempeh
1 Tbsp. ketchup
1 Tbsp. miso
1 tsp. onion powder
½ tsp. garlic powder
½ tsp. sage
½ tsp. thyme
⅛ tsp. cracked red pepper

1. Steam the tempeh for 20 minutes.

2. Process all the ingredients in a food processor until smooth and spreadable.

Per ¼ Cup: Calories: 92, Total Protein: 8 gm., Soy Protein: 7 gm., Fat: 4 gm., Carbohydrates: 8 gm., Calcium: 38 mg., Fiber 2 gm., Sodium: 168 mg.

TOFU CALIFORNIA DIP

Here is a tofu version of the dry onion soup mix dip. Serve with raw vegetables or chips.

1-10.5 oz. pkg. silken tofu
1 pkg. dry onion soup mix

1. Combine all the ingredients in a food processor or blender until creamy. Refrigerate overnight to let the flavors blend.

Per 2 Tbsp.: Calories: 24, Total Protein: 3 gm., Soy Protein: 2 gm., Fat: 0 gm., Carbohydrates: 2 gm., Calcium: 5 mg., Fiber 0 gm., Sodium: 240 mg.

TOFU-MISO-DILL DIP OR SPREAD

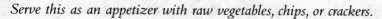

YIELD: 1½ CUPS

Serve this as an appetizer with raw vegetables, chips, or crackers.

½ lb. tofu
6 Tbsp. sweet yellow miso
3 Tbsp. rice vinegar
1 clove garlic, minced
1 tsp. dill weed

1. Combine all the ingredients in a food processor or blender until smooth and creamy.

Per 2 Tbsp.: Calories: 40, Total Protein: 3 gm., Soy Protein: 3 gm., Fat: 1 gm., Carbohydrates: 4 gm., Calcium: 31 mg., Fiber 1 gm., Sodium: 2 mg.

MISO HONEY MUSTARD
DRESSING OR DIP

Yield: ¾ cup

Serve with salad as a dressing or as a dip with raw vegetables.

¼ cup sweet yellow miso
¼ cup rice vinegar
2 Tbsp. soy oil
1 Tbsp. honey
¼ tsp. dry mustard

1. Combine all the ingredients in a blender until smooth and creamy.

Per 2 Tbsp.: Calories: 76, Total Protein: 1 gm., Soy Protein: 1 gm., Fat: 5 gm., Carbohydrates: 7 gm., Calcium: 8 mg., Fiber 1 gm., Sodium: 0 mg.

TARTAR SAUCE

YIELD: 1¾ CUPS

Serve Tartar Sauce *with* Oven Fried Tofu *(page 114)*, Tempeh Sticks *(page 38)*, *or* Soy Burgers *(page 60)*.

1-10.5 oz. pkg. silken tofu
2 Tbsp. lemon juice
2 tsp. onion powder
½ tsp. dry mustard
½ tsp. salt
6 Tbsp. onion, chopped
3 Tbsp. sweet pickle relish

1. Combine the tofu, lemon juice, onion powder, mustard, and salt in a blender until smooth and creamy. Fold in the onion and pickle relish.

Per 2 Tbsp.: Calories: 15, Total Protein: 2 gm., Soy Protein: 2 gm., Fat: 0 gm., Carbohydrates: 2 gm., Calcium: 2 mg., Fiber 0 gm., Sodium: 118 mg.

THOUSAND ISLAND DRESSING: Add ¼ cup ketchup when blending the ingredients together.

Per 2 Tbsp.: Calories: 19, Total Protein: 2 gm., Soy Protein: 2 gm., Fat: 0 gm., Carbohydrates: 2 gm., Calcium: 3 mg., Fiber 0 gm., Sodium: 163 mg.

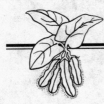

ZIPPY TOFU SALAD
DRESSING
Yield: 1½ cups

This is a replacement for mayonnaise that has no added fat. It has a zippy bite to it that adds a zing to sandwiches and salads. It will keep in the refrigerator for about a week. This recipe is from Lighten Up—With Louise Hagler.

1-10.5 oz. pkg. reduced-fat silken tofu
2 Tbsp. apple cider vinegar
1 Tbsp. sweetener of your choice
½ tsp. salt
⅛ tsp. dry mustard
¼ tsp. garlic powder

1. Combine all the ingredients in a blender or food processor until smooth and creamy.

Per 2 Tbsp.: Calories: 16, Total Protein: 2 gm., Soy Protein: 2 gm., Fat: 0 gm., Carbohydrates: 1 gm., Calcium: 1 mg., Fiber 0 gm., Sodium: 112 mg.

SOUP & SALAD

MISO SOMEN SOUP

Yield: 6 cups

This is a light, savory noodle soup in a classic Asian style.

¼ lb. somen
1 quart water
6" piece kombu (opt.)
1 medium carrot (1 cup), cut into matchstick pieces
¼ lb. tofu, cubed
6-8 scallions, chopped
6 Tbsp. sweet white miso

1. Cook the somen until tender, rinse, and drain.

2. Heat the water to boiling, add the kombu, and simmer about 5 minutes. Remove the kombu and save for use another time.

3. Add the carrot and simmer until just tender, about 5 minutes.

4. Add the somen, tofu, and half the scallions. Continue to simmer until all are hot.

5. Dip out about 1 cup of the broth, and dissolve the miso. Turn off the soup pot, and stir in the dissolved miso. Serve in soup bowls garnished with the rest of the scallions.

Per Cup: Calories: 87, Total Protein: 5 gm., Soy Protein: 3 gm., Fat: 1 gm., Carbohydrates: 12 gm., Calcium: 45 mg., Fiber 2 gm., Sodium: 11 mg.

MISO-TOFU SOUP

YIELD: 6–8 SERVINGS

You can try different flavors of miso to vary the taste of this soup.

6 cups water
1 carrot, cut in match stick size pieces
1 small onion, cut in rounds
½ lb. watercress, coarsely chopped
½ cup sweet white miso
½ lb. tofu,
    or ½ pkg. silken tofu, cut in small cubes

1. Bring the water to a boil, and add the carrot.

2. Turn off heat and add the onion, watercress, and tofu.

3. Dip out ½ cup hot water from the pot, and mix together with the miso.

4. Continue stirring until the mixture is smooth, then pour it back into the soup pot, and stir. Do not boil. Serve immediately.

Per Serving: Calories: 79, Total Protein: 5 gm., Soy Protein: 4 gm., Fat: 2 gm., Carbohydrates: 9 gm., Calcium: 92 mg., Fiber 2 gm., Sodium: 20 mg.

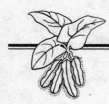

GREEN SOYBEAN SOUP

YIELD: 6 CUPS

Make this soup with either green soybeans when available or pressure cooked dried soybeans.

6 cups water
1 lb. green soybeans, shelled (2 cups shelled soybeans)
1 small onion, chopped
2 cloves garlic, minced
1 cup carrots, chopped
1 tsp. salt
¼ cup cilantro, chopped,
    or ¼ tsp. tarragon

1. Boil the green soybean in the water for 20 minutes.

2. Add the onion, garlic, carrots, and salt, and simmer until the carrots are tender. Stir in the cilantro, simmer a few more minutes, and serve hot.

Per Cup: Calories: 103, Total Protein: 8 gm., Soy Protein: 8 gm., Fat: 2 gm., Carbohydrates: 11 gm., Calcium: 103 mg., Fiber 2 gm., Sodium: 366 mg.

THREE BEAN SOUP

Yield: 8 cups

This is a hearty soup. Use leftover or canned beans for a quick meal.

1 medium onion, chopped
3 cloves garlic, minced
1 medium green pepper, chopped
3 cups water
1 cup crushed tomatoes or tomato sauce
1 cup cooked soybeans
1 cup cooked black beans
1 cup cooked kidney beans
1 tsp. oregano
1 bay leaf
1½ tsp. salt
⅛ tsp. allspice
⅛ tsp. chipotle

1. Sauté the onion, garlic, and green pepper in the oil just until tender.

2. Stir in the rest of the ingredients, and heat to boiling. Simmer a few minutes and serve.

Per Cup: Calories: 112, Total Protein: 7 gm., Soy Protein: 3 gm., Fat: 1 gm., Carbohydrates: 16 gm., Calcium: 47 mg., Fiber 4 gm., Sodium: 587 mg.

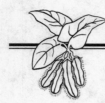

SOY CREAM OF CELERY

SOUP

Yield: 5 cups

This subtle, creamy soup is blended instead of strained, keeping all the fiber of the vegetables.

½ cup (¼ lb.) onion, chopped
4 cups (1 lb.) celery, chopped
2 cloves garlic, minced
½ Tbsp. soy or olive oil
2 cups stock or water
1½ tsp. salt
¼ tsp. dill
1 cup soymilk

1. Sauté the onion, celery, and garlic in the oil. Add the stock and simmer until soft.

2. Blend with a hand blender or in an electric blender until creamy. Return to the soup pot, stir in the salt, dill, and soymilk, and heat until almost boiling. Do not boil. Serve hot, garnished with chopped green onions or a sprig of fresh dill.

Per Serving: Calories: 48, Total Protein: 2 gm., Soy Protein: 1 gm., Fat: 2 gm., Carbohydrates: 5 gm., Calcium: 44 mg., Fiber 2 gm., Sodium: 726 mg.

SOY CREAM OF POTATO SOUP

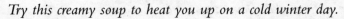

YIELD: 5 CUPS

Try this creamy soup to heat you up on a cold winter day.

2 cups (1 lb.) potatoes, cubed
1½ cups (½ lb.) onions, chopped
3 cloves garlic, minced
½ Tbsp. soy or olive oil
2 cups potato water, vegetable stock, or water
¼ cup (¼ oz.) fresh parsley, chopped
1 tsp. salt
¼ tsp. cracked red pepper or black pepper
1 cup soymilk
1 tsp. garlic flavored olive oil
fresh parsley, chopped

1. Boil the potatoes until soft, and reserve the cooking water.

2. Sauté the onions and garlic in the oil.

3. Add the potato water and potatoes, and blend with a hand blender or in a blender.

4. Return to the soup pot, and stir in the parsley, salt, red pepper, and soymilk. Heat until almost boiling, but do not boil. Serve garnished with a teaspoon of garlic flavored olive oil and chopped parsley.

Per Cup: Calories: 133, Total Protein: 3 gm., Soy Protein: 1 gm., Fat: 3 gm., Carbohydrates: 23 gm., Calcium: 30 mg., Fiber 3 gm., Sodium: 440 mg.

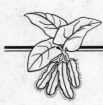

MISO VEGETABLE SOUP

YIELD: ABOUT 8 CUPS

You can use any vegetables you have on hand for this soup.

1 medium onion, chopped
2 cloves garlic, minced
1 stalk celery, chopped
1 carrot, chopped
1 Tbsp. soy or olive oil
5 cups water
1 bay leaf
1 cup fresh or frozen green beans, chopped
1 cup fresh or frozen corn
1 cup fresh or frozen broccoli, chopped
1 cup cooked soybeans
2 Tbsp. fresh parsley, chopped
¼ cup sweet barley miso

1. In a soup pot, sauté the onion, garlic, celery, and carrot in the oil until the onion is transparent.

2. Add the water, bay leaf, green beans, corn, broccoli, soybeans, and parsley, and simmer until the vegetables are tender.

3. Turn off the heat and stir in the miso. Serve hot with bread or crackers.

Per Cup: Calories: 111, Total Protein: 5 gm., Soy Protein: 4 gm., Fat: 4 gm., Carbohydrates: 13 gm., Calcium: 69 mg., Fiber 4 gm., Sodium: 19 mg.

ASIAN GREEK SALAD

Yield: 6 to 8 servings

This salad combines Asian, Greek, and south of the border flavors. This recipe is adapted from the Greek Salad in Tofu Cookery.

¼ cup olive oil
2 Tbsp. wine vinegar
2 Tbsp. miso
¼ tsp. freshly ground black pepper
2 cloves garlic
2 Tbsp. fresh basil, chopped
1 Tbsp. fresh oregano, chopped
1 lb. firm tofu, cut in ½" cubes
1 head leaf lettuce
2 fresh tomatoes, cubed
2 cucumbers, cubed
1 avocado, cubed
½ small red onion, chopped
½ cup Greek or black olives

1. Blend the olive oil, vinegar, miso, black pepper, and garlic. Stir in the basil and oregano.

2. Pour the dressing over the tofu cubes in a glass or stainless steel bowl, and marinate at least 1 hour or overnight.

3. Wash and dry the lettuce, and arrange in a salad bowl. Toss all the rest of the ingredients together, and serve in the lettuce lined bowl.

Per Serving: Calories: 219, Total Protein: 6 gm., Soy Protein: 5 gm., Fat: 16 gm., Carbohydrates: 12 gm., Calcium: 113 mg., Fiber 4 gm., Sodium: 85 mg.

TEMPEH-PASTA SALAD

This tasty salad is very simple to put together, despite its long list of ingredients. It makes a cool summer salad entrée.

8 oz. tempeh
2 Tbsp. water
1 Tbsp. soy sauce
1 Tbsp. wine or balsamic vinegar
½ Tbsp. soy or olive oil
1 clove garlic, minced
¼ tsp. oregano
½ lb. rotini pasta
1 medium tomato, chopped
½ cup celery, sliced
½ cup sweet yellow bell pepper, chopped
⅓ cup onion, chopped
¼ cup black olives, sliced
½ cup fresh basil, chopped,
   or 2 tsp. dried basil
¼ cup fresh parsley, chopped,
   or 1 tsp. dried parsley
3 Tbsp. olive oil
3 Tbsp. wine or balsamic vinegar
1 clove garlic, minced
½ tsp. salt
¼ tsp. freshly ground black pepper

1. Steam the tempeh for 20 minutes. Cut into ¼" thick by ½" long pieces.

2. Mix together the water, 1 Tbsp. soy sauce, 1 Tbsp. vinegar, ½ Tbsp. oil, 1 clove garlic, and oregano. Pour over the tempeh and toss to evenly distribute. Brown on both sides in a non-stick skillet.

3. Cook the pasta in boiling water until tender, rinse, and drain.

4. In a salad bowl, mix together the tomato, celery, bell pepper, onion, olives, basil, parsley, 3 Tbsp. olive oil, 3 Tbsp. vinegar, 1 clove garlic, salt, and black pepper. Add the browned tempeh and pasta, toss, and serve.

Per Cup: Calories: 159, Total Protein: 6 gm., Soy Protein: 5 gm., Fat: 8 gm., Carbohydrates: 14 gm., Calcium: 43 mg., Fiber 2 gm., Sodium: 299 mg.

TOFU PASTA SALAD: Substitute ½ lb. firm tofu for the tempeh.

Per Cup: Calories: 124, Total Protein: 4 gm., Soy Protein: 2 gm., Fat: 8 gm., Carbohydrates: 9 gm., Calcium: 46 mg., Fiber 1 gm., Sodium: 300 mg.

THAI NOODLE SALAD

YIELD: 8–9 CUPS

Add fresh hot pepper to this salad to make it as fiery as you like.

8 oz. tempeh
8 oz. soba or angel hair noodles
2 Tbsp. water
1 Tbsp. lime juice or rice vinegar
1 Tbsp. soy sauce
2 tsp. gingerroot, grated
⅛ tsp. cracked red pepper or hot pepper of choice
½ Tbsp. soy or peanut oil
2 cups carrot, grated
1 cup celery, thinly sliced
½ cup cilantro, chopped
½ cup green onion, chopped
¼ cup peanuts, chopped
2 Tbsp. lime juice
2 Tbsp. sweetener of choice
1 Tbsp. soy sauce
2 tsp. toasted sesame or peanut oil
1 tsp. gingerroot, grated
1 clove garlic, minced

1. Steam the tempeh for 20 minutes. Cut into ¼" x ½" pieces.

2. Cook the pasta in boiling water until tender, rinse, and drain.

3. Mix together the water, 1 Tbsp. lime juice, 1 Tbsp. soy sauce, 2 tsp. gingerroot, and red pepper. Pour over the tempeh pieces and toss to distribute the sauce evenly. Brown in a non-stick skillet with the ½ Tbsp. oil.

4. In a salad bowl, mix together the carrots, celery, cilantro, green onion, peanuts, 2 Tbsp. lime juice, sweetener, 1 Tbsp. soy

sauce, 2 tsp.oil, 1 tsp. gingerroot, and 1 clove garlic. Add the browned tempeh and the pasta, toss, and serve.

Per Cup: Calories: 206, Total Protein: 10 gm., Soy Protein: 5 gm., Fat: 6 gm., Carbohydrates: 27 gm., Calcium: 61 mg., Fiber 3 gm., Sodium: 279 mg.

TUNEMPEH SALAD

YIELD: 3 CUPS (4 SERVINGS)

This can be served in a sandwich, in a pita bread, stuffed in a tomato or avocado, or on a bed of lettuce.

8 oz. tempeh
1 cup Zippy Tofu Salad Dressing (page 76)
½ cup celery, diced
¼ cup green onions
2 tsp. sweet pickle relish
2 Tbsp. fresh parsley, minced
½ tsp. salt
⅛ tsp. freshly ground black pepper

1. Steam the tempeh for 20 minutes, then cut into ¼" cubes.

2. Mix all the ingredients together in a bowl, and serve.

Per Serving: Calories: 153, Total Protein: 13 gm., Soy Protein: 13 gm., Fat: 5 gm., Carbohydrates: 15 gm., Calcium: 70 mg., Fiber 4 gm., Sodium: 528 mg.

EGGLESS TOFU-POTATO
SALAD

YIELD: ABOUT 4½ CUPS (4–6 SERVINGS)

This is a summer picnic pleaser.

1½ lbs. potatoes
½ cup green onions, chopped
½ cup celery, chopped
¼ cup parsley, chopped
½ lb. soft tofu
3 Tbsp. apple cider vinegar
1½ Tbsp. sweetener of choice
½ tsp. salt
½ tsp. freshly ground black pepper
½ tsp. turmeric
½ cup pickles, chopped (opt.)

1. Wash and steam or boil the potatoes until tender. You can peel them or not according to taste, and cut into cubes.

2. In a blender, blend the tofu, vinegar, sweetener, salt, pepper, and turmeric until creamy.

3. Mix everything together in a bowl, chill, and serve.

Per Serving: Calories: 178, Total Protein: 5 gm., Soy Protein: 3 gm., Fat: 1 gm., Carbohydrates: 35 gm., Calcium: 76 mg., Fiber 4 gm., Sodium: 239 mg.

EGGLESS TOFU SALAD

Yield: about 3 cups (4 servings)

This versatile salad can make a sandwich, stuff a pita, top a bed of lettuce or tomato, or serve as a dip or spread with vegetables, chips, or crackers.

½ lb. soft tofu
3 Tbsp. apple cider vinegar
1½ Tbsp. sweetener of choice
1 tsp. onion powder
1 tsp. turmeric
½ tsp. salt
½ tsp. garlic powder
½ lb. firm tofu
½ cup celery, chopped
½ cup carrot, finely grated (opt.)
½ cup cucumber, chopped (opt.)
¼ cup onion, chopped
¼ cup parsley, chopped

1. In a blender or food processor, blend ½ lb. soft tofu, vinegar, sweetener, onion powder, turmeric, salt, and garlic powder until smooth.

2. Crumble ½ lb. firm tofu into a bowl. Mix in the celery, carrot, cucumber, onion, and parsley. Stir in the blended tofu mixture, and serve.

Per Serving: Calories: 108, Total Protein: 7 gm., Soy Protein: 7 gm., Fat: 4 gm., Carbohydrates: 11 gm., Calcium: 89 mg., Fiber 1 gm., Sodium: 294 mg.

SOY FOUR BEAN SALAD

Yield: 5 cups (6 servings)

This is a hearty, cool main dish to serve on a hot day. You can substitute any type of cooked beans you like or have on hand for the black beans and red beans.

1 cup cooked soybeans
1 cup cooked black beans
1 cup cooked red beans
1 cup cooked green beans
½ cup onion, chopped
½ cup celery, chopped
2 cloves garlic, minced
2 Tbsp. balsamic vinegar
2 Tbsp. soy or olive oil
2 Tbsp. fresh parsley, chopped
½ tsp. oregano
1 tsp. salt
¼ tsp. freshly ground black pepper

1. Toss all the ingredients together, refrigerate, and marinate overnight. Serve cold on a bed of lettuce.

Per Serving: Calories: 182, Total Protein: 9 gm., Soy Protein: 4 gm., Fat: 7 gm., Carbohydrates: 20 gm., Calcium: 72 mg., Fiber 5 gm., Sodium: 370 mg.

MAIN DISHES

BARBECUE TOFU

YIELD: 4–6 SERVINGS

This barbecue freezes well, so it's a good one to make a double or triple recipe and freeze some for later. You can bake it in the oven or grill it on the barbecue grill.

**2 cups your favorite prepared barbecue sauce
  or see Barbecue Soybeans (page 59)
1 lb. frozen tofu, thawed
soy or olive oil for the pan**

1. Preheat the oven to 350°F.

2. Squeeze the water out of the tofu, and cut into 8-12 rib sized pieces.

3. Spread a 9″ x 13″ pan with oil and arrange the tofu pieces on the pan leaving about ½″ between each piece. Bake about10 minutes until the tofu starts to brown. Turn the pieces over and bake about 10 minutes. Spread the barbecue sauce over the tofu, and bake for about 10 minutes more. Serve with French bread or potatoes and a crisp green salad.

Per Serving: Calories: 229, Total Protein: 6 gm., Soy Protein: 6 gm., Fat: 4 gm., Carbohydrates: 41 gm., Calcium: 102 mg., Fiber 7 gm., Sodium: 1619 mg.

BARBECUE TEMPEH

Fire up the grill or bake it in the oven.

8 oz. tempeh
1 cup you favorite barbecue sauce
   or see Barbecue Soybeans (page 59)

1. Steam the tempeh for 20 minutes.

2. Preheat the oven to 350°F, or prepare coals for grilling. Cut the tempeh into ¼" to ½" slices, strips, or chunks, and lay on a baking sheet. Spread the barbecue sauce over the tempeh pieces.

3. Bake for about 15 minutes, or until hot, or heat thoroughly on the grill, basting with more barbecue sauce.

Per Serving: Calories: 170, Total Protein: 7 gm., Soy Protein: 7 gm., Fat: 3 gm., Carbohydrates: 28 gm., Calcium: 45 mg., Fiber 6 gm., Sodium: 809 mg.

JERK TEMPEH OR TOFU

YIELD 4–6 SERVINGS

Jerk is a Jamaican way of spicing food that usually involves very hot peppers among other spices. A prepared Jerk Sauce can be used, or try the one below, and adjust the heat to your own taste. Scotch Bonnet pepper is the one used in Jamaica, but it is extremely hot on the hot pepper scale. A little jalapeño works for hot pepper wimps like me.

¼ cup apple or papaya juice
3 Tbsp. onion, grated
3 cloves garlic, minced
2 Tbsp. soy sauce
2 Tbsp. fresh hot pepper of choice, minced
2 Tbsp. vinegar
1 Tbsp. oil
1 Tbsp. gingerroot, grated
1½ tsp. allspice
½ tsp. cinnamon
½ tsp. freshly ground black pepper
½ tsp. thyme
¼ tsp. nutmeg
½ cup scallions, chopped
1 lb. steamed tempeh or tofu frozen , thawed, and squeezed
    dry

1. Mix all the dry ingredients together, except the scallions and tempeh.

2. Cut the tempeh or tofu into 1" cubes or ½" strips, and arrange one layer deep in a glass pan. Pour the blended mixture over the top. Press the sauce into the tofu with a spatula or the palm of your hands. Let it marinate for a few hours or overnight.

3. Preheat the oven to broil, prepare the coals in the grill, or heat the griddle.

4. Broil for about 5 minutes, turn the pieces over, and broil 5 more minutes. If you are cooking on a grill or oiled griddle, brown on both sides. Serve hot with chopped scallions for garnish.

Per Serving (with tempeh): Calories: 222, Total Protein: 18 gm.,
Soy Protein: 18 gm., Fat: 9 gm., Carbohydrates: 19 gm., Calcium: 98 mg.,
Fiber 5 gm., Sodium: 409 mg.

Per Serving (with tofu): Calories: 110, Total Protein: 7 gm., Soy Protein: 7 gm.,
Fat: 7 gm., Carbohydrates: 5 gm., Calcium: 109 mg., Fiber 1 gm.,
Sodium: 410 mg.

SWEET-SOUR TEMPEH
KEBABS

YIELD: 8 KEBABS

Cook these tangy, colorful kebabs in the oven or on the grill. This recipe is featured on the cover. Try mixing tempeh and frozen tofu to make these kebabs.

8 oz. tempeh, steamed
1 green pepper
1 sweet red pepper
1 medium onion
1 zucchini
2 apples or star fruit

For the Marinade:
1½ cups apple juice
6 Tbsp. cider vinegar
¼ cup honey
2 Tbsp. soy sauce
2 Tbsp. gingerroot, grated
4 cloves garlic, minced
2 Tbsp. cornstarch or arrowroot

1. Cut the tempeh and vegetables into ¾" chunks. Cut the fruit into thick slices. In a glass or stainless steel pan, spread everything out, one layer thick.

2. Whip together the marinade ingredients. **Microwave Method:** In a glass bowl, microwave the marinade on high for 6 minutes, stopping to whip every 2 minutes. **Stovetop Method:** In a saucepan, heat the marinade over medium heat, stirring constantly until it boils and starts to thicken. Reduce the heat and simmer for 2-3 minutes.

3. Pour over the marinade and vegetable chunks. Marinate in the refrigerator for a few hours to overnight.

4. Preheat the grill or oven to 400°F.

5. Arrange the tempeh and vegetables on skewers, then arrange on a pan or on the grill. Brush with the marinade and bake or grill for 15 to 20 minutes on each side or until browned. Serve the kebabs on a bed of brown rice, noodles, or millet. Heat the remaining sauce and pour over the top of the kebabs.

Per Serving: Calories: 163, Total Protein: 7 gm., Soy Protein: 6 gm., Fat: 2 gm., Carbohydrates: 22 gm., Calcium: 48 mg., Fiber 4 gm., Sodium: 258 mg.

SWEET-SOUR TOFU KEBABS: Use ½ lb. frozen tofu which has been thawed and squeezed dry in place of the tempeh.

Per Serving: Calories: 124, Total Protein: 3 gm., Soy Protein: 2 gm., Fat: 1 gm., Carbohydrates: 25 gm., Calcium: 29 mg., Fiber 2 gm., Sodium: 265 mg.

ENCHILADAS

This is a quick and easy recipe that freezes well if you have leftovers or want to cook ahead.

1 recipe Taco or Burrito Filling (page 106)

For the Chili Gravy:
1 medium onion, chopped
1 medium green pepper, chopped
2 cloves garlic, minced
½ Tbsp. oil or 2 Tbsp. water
6 Tbsp. unbleached white flour
1-2 Tbsp. chili powder, or to taste
¼ tsp. chipotle
½ tsp. salt
3 cups water

8-5″ corn tortillas

½ cup fresh cilantro, chopped

1. ***Chili Gravy—Microwave Method:*** Microwave the onion, green pepper, and garlic in the oil or water for 1 minute. In a 2-quart microwave bowl, whip together the flour, chili powder, chipotle, and salt. Whip in the water until smooth, then microwave on high for 6 minutes. Whip until smooth, microwave for 2 more minutes, and whip again. ***Stovetop Method:*** Sauté the onion, green pepper, and garlic in the oil until the onion is transparent. Mix together the flour, chili powder, chipotle, and salt, then stir into the sautéed vegetables. Whip in the water and simmer until thickened. Keep stirring with the whip to keep from forming lumps.

2. Pour about ⅓ of the Chili Gravy into an 11″ x 7″ glass baking pan. Dunk each tortilla into the Chili Gravy, then lay on a plate, and fill with about ⅓ cup of the Taco or Burrito Filling. Roll up each one and arrange in the pan. Pour the rest of the Chili Gravy

over the top, sprinkle the cilantro on top, and microwave for about 5 minutes or until heated all the way through, or bake in a 350°F oven about 25 minutes until heated through.

Per Serving: Calories: 252, Total Protein: 13 gm., Soy Protein: 9 gm., Fat: 6 gm., Carbohydrates: 36 gm., Calcium: 143 mg., Fiber 4 gm., Sodium: 624 mg.

YUBA PASTRAMI

Yield: about 5 cups (6–8 servings)

Try this spicy filling hot in a sandwich or with toasted bagels.

6 oz. dried bean curd sticks (yuba)
¾ cup onion, minced
2 cloves garlic, minced
1 Tbsp. olive oil
2 Tbsp. red wine vinegar
2 Tbsp. soy sauce
2 tsp. gingerroot, grated
2 tsp. paprika
¼ tsp. cloves or allspice
3 Tbsp. nutritional yeast
1 tsp. freshly ground black pepper

1. Break the bean curd sticks into 2 to 3-inch pieces, and soak in warm water until soft, about 1 hour, or boil about 20 minutes.

2. Sauté the onion and garlic in the olive oil until soft. Add the soaked bean curd sticks (yuba), vinegar, soy sauce, ginger, paprika, and cloves. Simmer until all the liquid evaporates, then stir in the nutritional yeast and black pepper.

Per Serving: Calories: 149, Total Protein: 12 gm., Soy Protein: 11 gm., Fat: 7 gm., Carbohydrates: 8 gm., Calcium: 61 mg., Fiber 0 gm., Sodium: 305 mg.

POT PIE

Steaming hot from the oven, this is a wintertime favorite in our house. I freeze any leftovers, wrapped as individual servings, ready to heat up for a quick meal.

1 Tbsp. soy sauce
⅞ cup boiling water
2 oz. chunk textured vegetable protein
½ recipe Creamy Country Gravy (page 40)
1½ cups (½ lb.) potatoes, cubed
1½ cups (½ lb.) carrots, cubed
½ cup water
½ large onion (1 cup), chopped
2 cloves garlic, minced
1 cup green peas, fresh or frozen
1 recipe Quick Soy Biscuits (page 41)

1. Mix the soy sauce into the boiling water, pour over the textured vegetable protein, and let stand for about 10 minutes.

2. Prepare the Creamy Country Gravy.

3. **Microwave Method:** Cook the potatoes and carrots in ½ cup water on high for 4 minutes. Add the onion and garlic, and microwave on high 3 more minutes. **Stovetop Method:** Steam or sauté the potatoes, carrots, onions, and garlic until just tender.

4. Preheat the oven to 400°F.

5. Mix together the cooked vegetables, their cooking water, the textured vegetable protein, gravy, and green peas, and pour into a 2-quart casserole.

6. Prepare the Quick Soy Biscuits, and roll out evenly to fit the top of the casserole.

7. Place the biscuit dough on top, and bake for about 30 minutes, or until the casserole is heated through and the biscuit dough is golden brown.

Per Serving: Calories: 202, Total Protein: 10 gm., Soy Protein: 7 gm., Fat: 6 gm., Carbohydrates: 26 gm., Calcium: 71 mg., Fiber 4 gm., Sodium: 198 mg.

VARIATIONS: Replace the textured vegetable protein with ½ lb. tempeh, which has been steamed and cubed, ½ lb. fresh tofu, cubed, or ½ lb. tofu, which has been frozen, thawed, squeezed dry, and cubed.

Per Serving (with tempeh): Calories: 230, Total Protein: 11 gm., Soy Protein: 8 gm., Fat: 8 gm., Carbohydrates: 28 gm., Calcium: 77 mg., Fiber 5 gm., Sodium: 198 mg.

Per Serving (with tofu): Calories: 199, Total Protein: 8 gm., Soy Protein: 5 gm., Fat: 8 gm., Carbohydrates: 25 gm., Calcium: 80 mg., Fiber 4 gm., Sodium: 198 mg.

TEMPEH CURRY

YIELD: 3½ CUPS (4–6 SERVINGS)

8 oz. tempeh
1 medium onion, chopped
2 cloves garlic, minced
1 Tbsp. oil
1-2 Tbsp. curry powder, or to taste
1 Tbsp. oil
2 Tbsp. unbleached white flour
3 cups soymilk
1 Tbsp. soy sauce
⅛ tsp. freshly ground black pepper
½ cup cilantro, chopped

1. Steam the tempeh for 20 minutes, and cut into ½" x ¼" pieces.

2. Sauté the onion and garlic in 1 Tbsp. oil over low heat until soft. Add the curry powder and tempeh, and simmer a few more minutes.

3. In another pan, heat 1 Tbsp. oil and the flour. Let them foam and cook together until the flour starts to brown. Whip in the soymilk until smooth, and continue to cook until thickened. Stir in the tempeh and onion mixture along with the soy sauce, black pepper, and cilantro. Serve hot over rice or millet.

Per Serving: Calories: 211, Total Protein: 14 gm., Soy Protein: 13 gm., Fat: 10 gm., Carbohydrates: 15 gm., Calcium: 66 mg., Fiber 5 gm., Sodium: 223 mg.

TOFU CURRY: Substitute the ½ lb. firm tofu or frozen tofu, thawed and squeezed dry for the tempeh. Cut the tofu into ½" x ¼" pieces.

Per Serving: Calories: 155, Total Protein: 8 gm., Soy Protein: 8 gm., Fat: 10 gm., Carbohydrates: 8 gm., Calcium: 71 mg., Fiber 3 gm., Sodium: 223 mg.

QUICK CHILI

Make this with textured vegetable protein or frozen tofu. A truly quick and easy meal, this would be a good one to serve anyone new to vegetarian protein.

2 cups water
2 cups cooked pinto beans,
   or 1-16 oz. can pinto beans
½ cup textured vegetable protein granules,
   or ½ lb. frozen tofu, thawed, squeezed dry, and torn or
   cubed
1-14 oz. can diced tomatoes or tomato sauce
½ cup green pepper, chopped
1 small onion, chopped,
   or 1 Tbsp. onion powder
1 clove garlic, crushed,
   or 1 tsp. garlic powder
1 Tbsp. chili powder
½ tsp. salt
½ cup fresh cilantro leaves, chopped (opt.)

1. Combine everything in a saucepan, and heat to boiling. Reduce to a simmer, cook for about 10 minutes, and serve.

Per Cup: Calories: 177, Total Protein: 12 gm., Soy Protein: 5 gm., Fat: 0 gm., Carbohydrates: 31 gm., Calcium: 91 mg., Fiber 7 gm., Sodium: 280 mg.

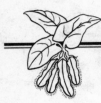

TACO OR BURRITO

FILLING

YIELD: 3 CUPS

This also makes a tasty filling for Enchiladas (page 100).

1 cup boiling water
2 Tbsp. soy sauce
1 Tbsp. chili powder
½ tsp. oregano
1 cup textured vegetable protein granules
½ cup onion, minced
½ cup green pepper, minced
1 clove garlic, minced
jalapeño to taste, minced (opt.)
1 Tbsp. olive oil

1. Mix together the boiling water, soy sauce, chili powder, and oregano, and pour over the textured vegetable protein granules. Cover and let stand for about 10 minutes.

2. Briefly sauté the onion, green pepper, garlic, and jalapeño in the olive oil. Add the textured vegetable protein mixture, and continue to cook until browned. Serve hot in tacos or burritos with all the fixings.

Per ½ Cup: Calories: 74, Total Protein: 7 gm., Soy Protein: 7 gm., Fat: 2 gm., Carbohydrates: 6 gm., Calcium: 39 mg., Fiber 2 gm., Sodium: 339 mg.

VARIATION: Add 1½ cups cooked pinto beans (1-16 oz can, drained) to the mixture, and simmer until heated.

Per ½ Cup: Calories: 133, Total Protein: 10 gm., Soy Protein: 7 gm., Fat: 2 gm., Carbohydrates: 17 gm., Calcium: 60 mg., Fiber 4 gm., Sodium: 340 mg.

SOY PROTEIN BALLS

This recipe is adapted from Lighten Up—With Louise Hagler.
Serve these balls with your favorite pasta and marinara sauce.

1 cup textured vegetable protein granules
⅞ cup boiling water
¼ cup unbleached white flour
1 small onion, diced,
   or 1 Tbsp. onion powder
1 clove garlic, minced,
   or ½ tsp garlic powder
½ tsp. salt
½ tsp. oregano
¼ tsp. basil
pinch of freshly ground black pepper
1 Tbsp. olive oil

1. Preheat the oven to 350°F.

2. Pour the boiling water over the textured vegetable protein granules. Let it stand for about 10 minutes, then fluff into a mixing bowl. Add the rest of the ingredients, except the oil, and mix well. Form into 16 balls.

3. Oil a baking sheet with the oil, and arrange the balls on the pan. Bake for 30 minutes, turning each ball every 10 minutes until lightly browned.

Per Ball: Calories: 27, Total Protein: 3 gm., Soy Protein: 3 gm., Fat: 0 gm.,
Carbohydrates: 3 gm., Calcium: 18 mg., Fiber 1 gm., Sodium: 68 mg.

TAMALES

Ask for fresh masa at you local tortillería or substitute masa flour for the tamale dough. Adding the okara adds more protein and fiber to the tamales. Making tamales can become a social event. Several families can do it together and make enough so everyone can feast and take some home to freeze for later.

½ lb. dried corn husks

For the Tofu Filling:
2 cloves garlic, minced
1 medium onion, chopped
½ poblano or green pepper, chopped
2 tsp. soy oil
1 lb. regular tofu, crumbled
1 Tbsp. chili powder
1½ tsp. salt
1 cup fresh cilantro, chopped

For the Masa Dough:
2 lbs. fresh masa
2 cups okara (opt.)
¼ cup soy oil (opt.)
2 tsp. salt or to taste

1. Soak the dried corn husks in water for about an hour to soften. Separate the husk, saving the larger ones to wrap the tamales, and put the smaller ones in the bottom of an 8-quart cooking pot to function as a steaming rack. Add about 2 to 3 inches of water to the pot.

2. **Tofu Filling:** Sauté the garlic, onion, and poblano in the oil until soft. Stir in the tofu, chili powder, salt, and cilantro.

3. Mix the masa, okara, oil, and salt with sufficient water to make a soft, easy to handle dough.

4. To assemble the tamales, use about ¼ cup masa dough to form a ball. Pat the ball into a tortilla shape about 3 inches round and ⅛" thick. Place 1 to 2 tablespoons filling in the center, fold the dough over, and seal around the filling to form a tamale. Place the tamale on the wide end of a corn husk, and roll it up. Fold under the empty end of the husk to hold it together. Stack the tamales loosely in the cooking pot to allow the steam to flow around them. Steam for one hour.

VARIATION: Try Taco or Burrito Filling with Beans (page 106) as the tamale filling.

---

*Per Tamale: Calories: 52, Total Protein: 2 gm., Soy Protein: 1 gm., Fat: 1 gm.,
Carbohydrates: 8 gm., Calcium: 26 mg., Fiber 2 gm., Sodium: 315 mg.*

SOY "SOUFFLE"

Soy "Souffle" was an entrée we served quite often on the early Farm, making as many seasonal variations as we could come up with. It is easy-to-make and hearty. It fluffs up but falls very fast! This is the basic souffle. This recipe is adapted from The New Farm Vegetarian Cookbook.

1 cup soy flour
¼ cup nutritional yeast
½ tsp. garlic powder
2 tsp. onion powder
¼ tsp. turmeric
¼ tsp. salt
1½ cups soymilk
1 Tbsp. salad mustard

1. Preheat the oven to 350°F.

2. Mix all the dry ingredients together. Whip in the soymilk and mustard, and pour into an oiled loaf or souffle pan. Bake for 45 minutes or until browned.

Per Serving: Calories: 212, Total Protein: 18 gm., Soy Protein: 15 gm., Fat: 9 gm., Carbohydrates: 15 gm., Calcium: 82 mg., Fiber 5 gm., Sodium: 296 mg.

SOY PROTEIN-TOFU BURGERS

YIELD: 6 BURGERS

This juicy burger is pictured on the cover.

¾ cup boiling water
2 Tbsp. soy sauce
1 cup textured vegetable protein granules
¼ cup onion, chopped
¼ cup green pepper, chopped
1 clove garlic, minced
½ lb. firm tofu, mashed
¼ cup ketchup
1 Tbsp. Dijon mustard
¼ tsp. freshly ground black pepper
½ cup whole wheat flour
1 Tbsp. olive oil1.

1. Mix together the boiling water and soy sauce. Pour over the textured vegetable protein granules, cover, and let stand for about 10 minutes.

2. Mix together the onion, green pepper, and garlic in a microwave safe bowl, cover, and microwave on high for 1 minute.

3. Mix all the ingredients together, and form into 6 burgers. Oil a non-stick griddle with the olive oil, and brown the burgers on both sides. Let the burgers cool a few minutes before serving to firm up. Serve on toasted buns with all the fixings.

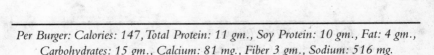

*Per Burger: Calories: 147, Total Protein: 11 gm., Soy Protein: 10 gm., Fat: 4 gm.,
Carbohydrates: 15 gm., Calcium: 81 mg., Fiber 3 gm., Sodium: 516 mg.*

TOFU-POTATO SOUFFLE

YIELD: 6 CUPS

Serve these savory, fluffy potatoes as a main dish or side dish.

2 lbs. russet potatoes
1 large onion, chopped
6 cloves garlic, minced
1 Tbsp. olive oil
1-10.5 oz. pkg. silken tofu
2 Tbsp. fresh parsley, chopped
1 tsp. salt
¼ tsp. freshly ground black pepper

1. Steam the potatoes until tender. Pull off the peels.

2. Sauté the onions and garlic in the olive oil until transparent.

3. Preheat the oven to 350°F.

4. Process the peeled potatoes and tofu in a food processor, or beat until smooth. Fold in the rest of the ingredients, and transfer to an oiled 2-quart casserole dish or loaf pan. Bake for 30 to 40 minutes until heated through and browned on top.

Per Cup: Calories: 102, Total Protein: 4 gm., Soy Protein: 3 gm., Fat: 4 gm., Carbohydrates: 13 gm., Calcium: 32 mg., Fiber 2 gm., Sodium: 377 mg.

ALMOND GRILLED TOFU

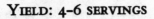

YIELD: 4–6 SERVINGS

This nutty flavored, chewy tofu makes a tasty appetizer, entrée, sandwich, or snack.

1½ lbs tofu, frozen, thawed, and squeezed dry
¼ cup water
2 Tbsp. almond butter
2 Tbsp. soy sauce
2 Tbsp. wine or balsamic vinegar
1 Tbsp. onion, grated
1 clove garlic, minced,
**   or ½ tsp. garlic powder**

1. Cut the prepared tofu into pieces ¼" x ½" x 2". Spread the pieces out in a pan.

2. In a blender, blend together the water, almond butter, soy sauce, vinegar, onion, and garlic. Pour the sauce evenly over the tofu. Gently squeeze the tofu so the sauce is evenly absorbed.

3. ***Oven Method:*** Preheat the oven to 350°F. Spread the tofu pieces on a lightly oiled cookie sheet, and bake for about 10 minutes. Turn the pieces over and bake about 5 minutes on the other side until browned. ***Stovetop Method:*** Brown the tofu pieces on a lightly oiled non-stick surface or over a grill.

Per Serving: Calories: 148, Total Protein: 11 gm., Soy Protein: 10 gm., Fat: 9 gm., Carbohydrates: 4 gm., Calcium: 162 mg., Fiber 1 gm., Sodium: 413 mg.

OVEN FRIED TOFU

YIELD: 4-6 SERVINGS

A quick and easy basic, this is one our kids favorites. It is delicious hot or cold. Serve it with steamed grains and vegetables or in a sandwich with all the fixings.

1 lb. firm tofu
6 Tbsp. unbleached white or whole wheat flour
3 Tbsp. nutritional yeast
2 tsp. onion powder
1 tsp. garlic powder
½ tsp. poultry seasoning
¼ tsp. freshly ground black pepper
1 Tbsp. soy sauce
1 Tbsp. oil

1. Preheat the oven to 400°F.

2. Slice the tofu ⅛" to ¼" thick.

3. Mix together the dry ingredients.

4. Dip the tofu in the soy sauce, then dredge in the flour mixture. Arrange on an oiled cookie sheet, and bake 10 minutes until browned on the bottom. Turn and bake about 5 more minutes until browned on the other side.

OVEN FRIED CHIPOTLE TOFU: Replace the poultry seasoning and black pepper with ¼ tsp. ground chipotle.

VARIATION: For a crunchier breading, replace the flour with finely ground cornmeal.

Per Serving: Calories: 140, Total Protein: 9 gm., Soy Protein: 7 gm., Fat: 6 gm., Carbohydrates: 10 gm., Calcium: 121 mg., Fiber 1 gm., Sodium: 214 mg.

LEMON GINGER TOFU
OR TEMPEH

YIELD: 8 SLICES (4 SERVINGS)

Enjoy the zest of lemon and ginger.

2 Tbsp. fresh lemon juice
½ Tbsp. organic lemon zest
2 Tbsp. soy sauce
1 Tbsp. onion, grated
1 clove garlic, pressed
½ Tbsp. fresh gingerroot, grated
1 lb. firm tofu, cut in 8 slices
2 tsp. sesame seeds

1. Mix together the lemon juice, zest, soy sauce, onion, garlic, and gingerroot. Arrange the tofu slices in one layer in a glass or stainless pan. Pour the lemon mixture over the tofu, and marinate from 2 to 24 hours.

2. ***Broiler Method:*** Preheat the broiler. Sprinkle the tofu slices with the sesame seeds, and broil 4 to 5 minutes until browned. ***Stovetop Method:*** Brown the tofu slices on both sides in a small amount of soy or olive oil. Sprinkle with sesame seeds and serve.

Per Serving: Calories: 116, Total Protein: 9 gm., Soy Protein: 9 gm., Fat: 7 gm., Carbohydrates: 4 gm., Calcium: 124 mg., Fiber 1 gm., Sodium: 511 mg.

VARIATION: Replace the tofu with 1 lb. tempeh that has been steamed for 20 minutes, and cut into ½" slices.

Per Serving: Calories: 256, Total Protein: 23 gm., Soy Protein: 23 gm., Fat: 10 gm., Carbohydrates: 21 gm., Calcium: 110 mg., Fiber 6 gm., Sodium: 510 mg.

HONEY-MUSTARD
NUGGETS

YIELD: 4 SERVINGS

Serve these tangy chewy nuggets with a salad or slaw.

1 lb. tofu, frozen, thawed, and squeezed dry
¼ cup water
¼ cup honey
¼ cup spicy or Dijon mustard
2 Tbsp. soy sauce or tamari
1 Tbsp. lemon juice
1 Tbsp. onion powder
1 tsp. garlic powder,
   or 1 clove garlic, minced

1. Preheat the oven to 350°F.

2. Cut the tofu into 1" x 1" x ½" pieces, and place in a shallow bowl or baking pan.

3. With a whip or in a food processor or blender, blend together the water, honey, mustard, soy sauce, lemon juice, onion powder, and garlic. Pour this mixture over the tofu pieces, and gently squeeze it in with the palm of your hand until it is evenly distributed and absorbed.

4. Spread out the tofu pieces one layer thick on an oiled baking sheet, and bake for about 10 minutes, or until they start to brown on the bottom. Flip the pieces over and bake about 5 to 10 more minutes. Serve hot.

Per Serving: Calories: 182, Total Protein: 9 gm., Soy Protein: 9 gm., Fat: 8 gm., Carbohydrates: 19 gm., Calcium: 122 mg., Fiber 0 gm., Sodium: 932 mg.

SLOPPY JOE

YIELD: 3 CUPS (6 SERVINGS)

Here is a quick meal that children love.

1 clove garlic, minced
1 medium onion, chopped
1 green pepper, chopped
1 tsp. soy or olive oil
2½ cups tomato sauce
1 tsp. chili powder
½ tsp. oregano
½ tsp. basil
½ tsp. salt
¼ tsp. freshly ground black pepper
1 lb. tofu, frozen, thawed, squeezed dry, and crumbled

1. Sauté the garlic, onion, and green pepper in the oil. Add the tomato sauce, chili powder, oregano, basil, salt, black pepper, and tofu. Heat until simmering. Serve as a sandwich over burger buns.

Per Serving: Calories: 108, Total Protein: 6 gm., Soy Protein: 5 gm., Fat: 4 gm., Carbohydrates: 10 gm., Calcium: 103 mg., Fiber 4 gm., Sodium: 801 mg.

VARIATION: Replace the frozen tofu with 1 cup textured vegetable protein granules soaked in ⅞ cup boiling water for 10 minutes.

Per Serving: Calories: 94, Total Protein: 8 gm., Soy Protein: 7 gm., Fat: 1 gm., Carbohydrates: 13 gm., Calcium: 57 mg., Fiber 5 gm., Sodium: 799 mg.

SOBA WITH TOFU AND PEANUTS

Yield: 4 servings

Serve this quick and easy, spicy dish with a cool green salad.

For the Marinade:
1 Tbsp. balsamic vinegar
2 Tbsp. soy sauce
2 tsp. fresh hot chile of choice, chopped
1 tsp. toasted sesame oil
1 Tbsp. fresh gingerroot, grated
1 clove garlic, minced

½ lb. firm tofu, cut in 1" x ¾" x ½" pieces

½ lb. soba noodles
½ cup fresh cilantro, chopped
¼ cup dry roasted peanuts
2 Tbsp. green onions, chopped

1. Mix the vinegar, soy sauce, chile, sesame oil, ginger, and garlic. Pour the mixture over the tofu pieces to marinate.

2. Boil the soba noodles until tender. Rinse in hot water and drain.

3. While the noodles are cooking, brown the tofu pieces on a non-stick grill, reserving the marinade. Toss the noodles and browned tofu together with the cilantro, peanuts, green onions, and the remaining marinade. Serve hot or cold.

Per Serving: Calories: 191, Total Protein: 10 gm., Soy Protein: 5 gm., Fat: 7 gm., Carbohydrates: 19 gm., Calcium: 81 mg., Fiber 4 gm., Sodium: 512 mg.

THAI TOFU IN PEANUT
SAUCE

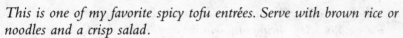

YIELD: 4–6 SERVINGS

This is one of my favorite spicy tofu entrées. Serve with brown rice or noodles and a crisp salad.

1 lb. tofu, frozen, thawed, and squeezed dry
4 cloves garlic
2" square fresh gingerroot
¼ cup peanuts
1 cup (2 oz.) cilantro leaves, loosely packed
¼ cup peanut butter
¼ cup soy sauce
¼ cup water
3 Tbsp. rice vinegar
3 Tbsp. honey
½ tsp. cracked red pepper flakes
2 green onions, chopped

1. Preheat the oven to 350°F.

2. Cut the tofu into ¼" thick slices.

3. In a food processor, chop the garlic, ginger, peanuts, and cilantro. Add the peanut butter, soy sauce, water, vinegar, honey, and cracked red pepper flakes, and blend until smooth.

4. Pour half of the sauce in a 7" x 11" baking pan. Lay the tofu slices on top, then pour the rest of the peanut sauce over the top. Press each slice so it absorbs the sauce. Bake for about 15 to 20 minutes, or until the slices start to brown. Sprinkle with green onions and serve hot with rice.

Per Serving: Calories: 243, Total Protein: 12 gm., Soy Protein: 8 gm., Fat: 12 gm., Carbohydrates: 19 gm., Calcium: 130 mg., Fiber 2 gm., Sodium: 818 mg.

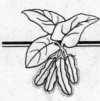

TOFU LOAF

YIELD: 6–8 SERVINGS

Serve this loaf hot with Creamy Country Gravy *(page 40) and mashed potatoes. Try slicing any leftover loaf for sandwiches.*

1½ lbs. firm tofu, mashed
½ cup wheat germ
½ cup fresh parsley, chopped
¼ cup onion, minced
1 clove garlic, minced
2 Tbsp. soy sauce
½ Tbsp. Dijon mustard
¼ tsp. freshly ground black pepper

1. Preheat the oven to 350°F.

2. Mix all the ingredients together, and press evenly into an oiled loaf pan. Bake for about 50 minutes, then let cool on a rack for 10 to 15 minutes before removing from the pan.

TOFU BURGERS: Form the mixture into 6 to 8 burgers, and brown on both sides in olive oil on a non-stick griddle. Let cool a few minutes to firm up before serving. Serve on toasted buns with all the fixings.

Per Serving: Calories: 114, Total Protein: 10 gm., Soy Protein: 7 gm., Fat: 5 gm., Carbohydrates: 6 gm., Calcium: 111 mg., Fiber 2 gm., Sodium: 326 mg.

TOFU SPINACH BALLS

YIELD: 48 ONE–INCH BALLS

These tasty balls are a welcome and colorful addition to pasta and marinara sauce. Try using baby kale leaves to substitute for the spinach. This recipe was adapted from a recipe given to me by Jo Anne Abercrombie.

2 cloves garlic
½ large onion
¼ cup walnuts, roasted and chopped
1 lb. spinach, frozen, thawed, and drained
1 lb. firm tofu
4 cups whole grain bread crumbs
1 Tbsp. soy sauce
1 tsp. sage or rosemary

1. Preheat the oven to 350°F.

2. Finely chop the garlic and onion in a food processor or by hand, and set aside in a mixing bowl. Chop the walnuts and spinach, and add to the bowl. Blend the tofu until creamy, and add. Add the bread crumbs, soy sauce, and sage, and mix.

3. Form the mixture into 48 one-inch balls, and arrange them on two oiled cookie sheets. Bake for 25 to 30 minutes or until browned. You can roll the balls about every 10 minutes to brown on several sides.

Per 2 Balls: Calories: 50, Total Protein: 3 gm., Soy Protein: 1 gm., Fat: 1 gm., Carbohydrates: 5 gm., Calcium: 60 mg., Fiber 1 gm., Sodium: 98 mg.

TOFU SPINACH PASTA
FILLING

YIELD: 5-6 CUPS (12 SERVINGS)

Use this filling for lasagne, stuffed pasta shells, or manicotti. Look for soy pasta, or use 12 Soy Crepes (page 42) to wrap around this savory filling.

1 lb. pasta
2-10.5 oz. pkgs. spinach
1 large onion, chopped
1 green pepper, chopped
4 cloves garlic, minced
1 Tbsp. olive oil
2 lbs. tofu
6 Tbsp. fresh lemon juice
1 tsp. salt
2 oz. fresh basil, chopped
4 cups marinara or pasta sauce

1. Preheat the oven to 350°F.

2. Cook the pasta according to package directions or prepare 12 Soy Crepes (page 42).

3. Thaw, drain, and chop the spinach. Sauté the onion, green pepper, and garlic in the olive oil.

4. In a food processor, blend the tofu, lemon juice, and salt. Fold in the chopped spinach, sautéed vegetables, and basil.

5. Fill or stuff the cooked pasta or Soy Crepes, and bake in your favorite marinara or pasta sauce for 40 minutes until bubbling and heated through.

Per Serving: Calories: 179, Total Protein: 9 gm., Soy Protein: 5 gm., Fat: 5 gm., Carbohydrates: 24 gm., Calcium: 170 mg., Fiber 5 gm., Sodium: 721 mg.

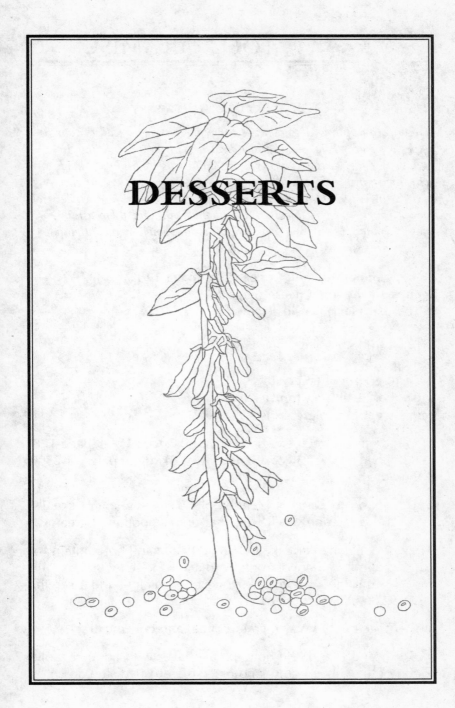

DESSERTS

TOFU TIRAMISU

YIELD: 10-12 SERVINGS

This rich and filling dessert needs to be made a day ahead of time. It serves a lot of people, making it a great dessert for entertaining. In Italian, tiramisu means "pick me up," and it is traditionally made with high-fat mascarpone cheese and cream. Tangy soy yogurt cheese and creamy silken tofu take the place of these high-fat, high-cholesterol foods to make a crowd pleasing dessert that will have them asking for more. Arrange tiramisu on a platter, in a trifle bowl, or in individual serving dishes.

½ recipe Sour Soymilk Cocoa Cake (page 128)
2 cups Soy Yogurt Cheese (page 152)
1-10.5 oz. pkg. firm silken tofu
1 cup sweetener of choice
1 tsp. vanilla
½ cup water
4 Tbsp. grain coffee crystals
1 tsp. coffee extract (opt.)
semi-sweet chocolate curls

1. Prepare half a recipe of Sour Soymilk Cocoa Cake (page 128) and bake in a 9" x 13" cake pan or two 8" round pans for 25 to 30 minutes.

2. In a food processor or blender, blend the soy yogurt cheese, tofu, sweetener, and vanilla together until smooth and creamy.

3. Cut the rectangular cake in half vertically and horizontally, or cut the rounds in half horizontally to make four equal layers. You can also cut the cake to fit a trifle bowl or individual serving dishes. You will need 4 equal layers of cake for each dish.

4. Mix together the water, grain coffee, and coffee extract.

5. Brush one side of the bottom cake layer with about 1 table-spoon of the coffee liquid, and place the brushed side down on

a platter or in a serving bowl. Brush the top of that cake layer with another tablespoon of the coffee liquid. Pour ¼ of the soy yogurt cheese and tofu mixture over the first cake layer and spread evenly. Repeat the layering for the next 3 layers. Cover and refrigerate for 24 hours or more for the flavors to meld. Sprinkle with the chocolate curls, and serve.

Per Serving: Calories: 313, Total Protein: 8 gm., Soy Protein: 5 gm., Fat: 7 gm., Carbohydrates: 52 gm., Calcium: 37 mg., Fiber 3 gm., Sodium: 167 mg.

CHOCOLATE TOFU
GANACHE

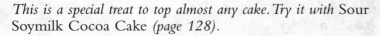

YIELD: ABOUT 2 CUPS

This is a special treat to top almost any cake. Try it with Sour Soymilk Cocoa Cake *(page 128).*

1-10.5 oz. pkg. silken tofu
3 Tbsp. corn syrup
6 oz. (1 cup) semi or bittersweet chocolate, chopped

1. Blend the tofu and corn syrup until smooth and creamy.

2. Microwave 2 minutes, whip, and microwave 1 more minute. Whip in the chocolate chips, let them melt, then whip again until smooth and blended.

3. Let the mixture cool, then whip and spread over cake. Chill until firm and serve.

Per ¼ Cup: Calories: 154, Total Protein: 5 gm., Soy Protein: 3 gm., Fat: 10 gm., Carbohydrates: 11 gm., Calcium: 27 mg., Fiber 2 gm., Sodium: 25 mg.

TOFU CHEESECAKE
BROWNIES

These rich, eggless brownies topped with tofu cheesecake will be well received at any gathering.

For the Brownie Layer:
⅔ cup soymilk
3 Tbsp. unbleached flour
¼ cup oil
½ cup cocoa
1 cup sweetener of choice
1 tsp. vanilla
1 cup unbleached flour
2 Tbsp. soy flour
1 tsp. baking powder
¼ tsp. salt

For the Cheesecake Layer:
1-10.5 oz. pkg. silken tofu
½ cup sweetener of choice
1 Tbsp. unbleached flour
1 Tbsp. lemon juice
2 tsp. vanilla

1. Preheat the oven to 350°F.

2. **Brownie Layer:** Whip together the soymilk and 3 Tbsp. flour. **Stovetop Method:** Cook over medium heat, stirring constantly until thickened. **Microwave Method:** Cook on high for 1 minute, whip, cook on high 1 more minute, and whip. Let cool completely.

3. Beat together the oil, cocoa, sweetener, and vanilla, then beat in the cooled soymilk and flour mixture. Add 1 cup flour, soy flour, baking powder, and salt, and beat until smooth. Oil your fingers and spread evenly into a 9" round spring form pan.

126

4. **_Cheesecake Layer:_** Blend the tofu, ½ cup sweetener, 1 Tbsp. flour, lemon juice, and 2 tsp. vanilla in a blender until smooth and creamy. Pour evenly over the brownie layer, and bake for 1 hour. Cool and serve.

Per Serving: Calories: 155, Total Protein: 4 gm., Soy Protein: 2 gm., Fat: 5 gm., Carbohydrates: 26 gm., Calcium: 22 mg., Fiber 2 gm., Sodium: 53 mg.

CREAMY TOFU TOPPING

YIELD: 1½ CUPS

This is a versatile, no cholesterol topping you can use to top many different sweet things.

1-10.5 oz. pkg. silken tofu
3 Tbsp. sweetener of choice
1 tsp. vanilla

1. Combine all the ingredients in a blender or food processor until smooth and creamy.

Per ¼ Cup: Calories: 49, Total Protein: 2 gm., Soy Protein: 2 gm., Fat: 1 gm., Carbohydrates: 7 gm., Calcium: 11 mg., Fiber 0 gm., Sodium: 3 mg.

SOUR SOYMILK COCOA CAKE

Yield: 1 bundt cake (16 servings)

Try topping this cake with Chocolate Tofu Ganache *(page 125) to make a combination that will satisfy any chocolate cravings. If you don't have sour soymilk, just add a tablespoon of lemon juice to your soymilk.*

2 cups unbleached white flour
1 cup whole wheat pastry flour
¼ cup soy flour
2½ tsp. baking soda
½ tsp. salt
¾ cup cocoa
6 Tbsp. oil
2 cups granulated sweetener
2 cups sour soymilk
2 tsp. vanilla, coffee, or mint extract

1. Preheat the oven to 350°F.

2. Mix the flours, soda, salt, and cocoa.

3. Beat together the oil, sweetener, sour soymilk, and vanilla. Add the dry ingredients and beat until smooth. Pour into an oiled 12-cup bundt pan, and bake for 45 to 50 minutes, or until the cake springs back to a light touch of the finger. Cool 15 minutes then remove from the pan.

Per Serving: Calories: 245, Total Protein: 5 gm., Soy Protein: 2 gm., Fat: 6 gm., Carbohydrates: 42 gm., Calcium: 37 mg., Fiber 4 gm., Sodium: 72 mg.

APPLESAUCE
CRANBERRY NUT CAKE

YIELD: 1 SMALL BUNDT CAKE (12 SERVINGS)

This makes a festive fruit cake for the holidays or any day of the year.

1½ cups whole wheat pastry flour
½ cup soy flour
1½ tsp. baking soda
½ tsp. salt
1½ tsp. cinnamon
½ tsp. ginger
¼ tsp. allspice or cloves
⅛ tsp. nutmeg
¼ cup oil
1½ cups granulated sweetener
1 cup unsweetened applesauce
1½ cups (6 oz.) cranberries
½ cup broken walnuts

1. Preheat the oven to 350°F.

2. Mix together the flours, baking soda, salt, and spices.

3. Beat together the oil, sweetener, and applesauce. Add the dry ingredient mixture, and beat until smooth. Fold in the cranberries and walnuts. Pour into an oiled, 6-cup bundt pan, and bake for about 50 minutes. Cool for about 15 minutes before removing from the pan.

Per Serving: Calories: 247, Total Protein: 4 gm., Soy Protein: 2 gm., Fat: 9 gm., Carbohydrates: 29 gm., Calcium: 18 mg., Fiber 4 gm., Sodium: 91 mg.

TOFU CRÈME-FILLED
ORANGE CRUMB CAKE

YIELD: 16 SERVINGS

This orange-crumb-topped, creamy-filled spice cake is put together in three layers. The recipe is adapted from Tofu Cookery.

For the First Layer:
1 cup unbleached flour
½ cup granulated sweetener of choice
2 Tbsp. oil
1½ Tbsp. organic orange zest
½ tsp. salt
½ cup walnuts, chopped

For the Second Layer:
1 lb. tofu
½ cup sweetener of choice
2 Tbsp. cornstarch
1 Tbsp vanilla
½ tsp. salt

For the Third Layer:
1½ cups soymilk
1 cup sweetener of choice
2 Tbsp. oil
4 Tbsp. orange juice
2 cups unbleached flour
½ cup walnuts, chopped
2 tsp. baking powder
½ tsp. baking soda
½ tsp. cinnamon
½ tsp. salt
⅛ tsp. nutmeg

1. Preheat the oven to 350°F.

2. *First Layer:* Combine the flour, sweetener, oil, orange zest, and salt in a food processor until blended. Add the walnuts and

process until chopped. Press the mixture into the bottom and up the sides of the bundt pan.

3. **Second Layer:** Blend the ingredients for the second layer together in a food processor or blender until smooth and creamy. Pour and spread on top of the first layer.

4. **Third layer:** Mix together the flour, walnuts, baking powder, baking soda, cinnamon, and salt. Beat together the soymilk, sweetener, oil, and orange juice, add the dry ingredients, and beat until smooth. Pour and spread this mixture over the second layer, being careful not to stir the second and third layers together. Bake for 40 to 45 minutes. Let cool 15 minutes, then loosen the edges, and turn out onto a rack to cool.

Per Serving: Calories: 247, Total Protein: 4 gm., Soy Protein: 2 gm., Fat: 9 gm., Carbohydrates: 29 gm., Calcium: 18 mg., Fiber 4 gm., Sodium: 91 mg.

APPLESAUCE SPICE
BUNDT CAKE

YIELD: ONE 6 CUP BUNDT CAKE
(12 SERVINGS)

If you have okara left from making soymilk, try it in this spicy cake.

1 cup unbleached white flour
1 cup whole wheat flour
1 tsp. baking powder
½ tsp. baking soda
1 tsp. cinnamon
¼ tsp. salt
¼ tsp. allspice
⅛ tsp. nutmeg
2 Tbsp. soy or canola oil
¾ cup honey or sweetener of choice
1 cup applesauce
1 cup okara
½ Tbsp. fresh gingerroot, finely chopped
¼ cup currants or raisins

1. Preheat the oven to 350°F.

2. Mix together all the dry ingredients.

3. In a mixer, mix together the oil, honey, applesauce, okara, and gingerroot until smooth and creamy.

4. Add the dry ingredients to the wet mixture, and beat until smooth. Beat in the currants.

5. Pour into a 6-cup bundt pan, and bake for 35 to 40 minutes. Let cool about 15 minutes before removing from the pan.

Per Serving: Calories: 169, Total Protein: 3 gm., Soy Protein: 0 gm., Fat: 3 gm., Carbohydrates: 33 gm., Calcium: 31 mg., Fiber 3 gm., Sodium: 48 mg.

KEY LIME PIE FILLING

Yield: filling for one 9" pie (8 servings)

This filling can be used a pie filling or served as pudding or parfait.

¾ cup fresh key lime juice
2½ cups soymilk
1 cup sweetener of choice
5 Tbsp. cornstarch
2 tsp. organic lime zest

1. Whip all the ingredients together until smooth.

2. **Microwave Method:** Pour in a 2-quart glass measuring cup or bowl, and cook on high 10 minutes, stopping to whip every 2 minutes. **Stovetop Method:** Whip all the ingredients together in a saucepan, and heat over moderate heat, stirring constantly until thick and creamy.

3. Pour into a baked pie crust or serving dishes, and chill until firm. Top with Creamy Tofu Topping (page 127) and decorate with lime slices.

Per Serving (filling only): Calories: 139, Total Protein: 2 gm., Soy Protein: 2 gm., Fat: 1 gm., Carbohydrates: 30 gm., Calcium: 5 mg., Fiber 1 gm., Sodium: 9 mg.

DOUBLE GINGER
COOKIES

YIELD: 48 THREE-INCH COOKIES

Bake these festive cut out cookies for the holidays or anytime for a treat.

½ lb. tofu
1 cup sorghum or molasses
¼ cup soy oil
¼ cup gingerroot, grated
3½ cups unbleached flour
½ cup soy flour
2 tsp. ginger
1 tsp. baking soda
1 tsp. cinnamon
½ tsp. salt
½ tsp. allspice

1. Blend the tofu, sorghum, oil, and gingerroot in a blender until smooth and creamy, and pour into a mixing bowl.

2. Mix the dry ingredients, and add to the mixing bowl.

3. Preheat the oven to 350°F.

4. Roll out he dough to ⅛" to ¼" thick, and cut with cookie cutters. Arrange on cookie sheets and bake 7 to 8 minutes until browned. Cool on racks and decorate as desired.

Per Cookie: Calories: 72, Total Protein: 2 gm., Soy Protein: 1 gm., Fat: 1 gm., Carbohydrates: 13 gm., Calcium: 29 mg., Fiber 0 gm., Sodium: 32 mg.

TOFFEE BARS

YIELD: 24 BARS

These chewy bars are a welcome variation on chocolate chip bars.

1 cup unbleached white flour
1 cup whole wheat pastry flour
¼ cup soymilk powder
1 tsp. baking powder,
    or ½ tsp baking soda and sour soymilk
½ tsp. salt
1½ cups granulated sweetener of choice
¼ cup oil
1 tsp. vanilla
½ cup soymilk
1 cup chocolate chips

1. Preheat the oven to 350°F.

2. Mix together the flours, soymilk powder, baking powder, and salt.

3. Beat together the sweetener, oil, and vanilla. Beat in the soymilk and the flour mixture until smooth. Spread the batter into an oiled 9″ x 13″ pan, and bake for 20 minutes. Sprinkle the chocolate chips evenly over the top of the hot bars. Let them sit for a few minutes until they start to melt, then spread evenly over the whole pan. Let it cool then cut into 24 bars.

*Per Bar: Calories: 141, Total Protein: 2 gm., Soy Protein: 1 gm., Fat: 5 gm.,
Carbohydrates: 23 gm., Calcium: 12 mg., Fiber 1 gm., Sodium: 46 mg.*

OKARA MACAROONS

YIELD: 24 COOKIES

These are moist and chewy, vegetarian, macaroon-like cookies.

1 cup unbleached white flour
½ cup whole wheat pastry flour
1½ tsp. baking soda
½ tsp. salt
1½ cups granulated sweetener
¼ cup oil
2 tsp. vanilla
2 cups okara

1. Preheat the oven to 350°F.

2. Mix the flours, baking soda, and salt.

3. Beat together the sweetener, oil, and vanilla. Beat in the okara and then the flour mixture.

4. Drop by tablespoon onto oiled cookie sheets, and bake about 10 to 12 minutes or until browned.

Per Cookie: Calories: 78, Total Protein: 1 gm., Soy Protein: 0 gm., Fat: 0 gm., Carbohydrates: 18 gm., Calcium: 17 mg., Fiber 1 gm., Sodium: 45 mg.

OKARA CHOCOLATE CHIP MACAROONS: Mix in ½ cup chocolate chips after beating in the flour mixture.

Per Cookie: Calories: 96, Total Protein: 1 gm., Soy Protein: 0 gm., Fat: 1 gm., Carbohydrates: 20 gm., Calcium: 18 mg., Fiber 1 gm., Sodium: 46 mg.

EASY MICROWAVE

TAPIOCA

YIELD: ABOUT 6 CUPS

Here is an old time favorite prepared by an updated method. If you don't have a microwave, you can cook it by the old fashioned double-boiler method.

½ cup small-medium pearl tapioca
1 cup soymilk
3 cups soymilk
1½ cups sweetener of choice, or to taste
2 tsp. vanilla

1. Soak ½ cup tapioca in 1 cup soymilk overnight.

2. Pour 3 cups soymilk into a 2-quart glass bowl or measuring cup. Add the soaked tapioca and sweetener with a whip. Microwave on high for 6 minutes, and stir thoroughly with a whip.

3. Microwave on high again for 2 minutes, whip, and microwave 2 more minutes. Don't let it boil over. Whip in the vanilla and pour into individual serving dishes or a serving bowl. Serve warm or chill and serve.

Per ½ Cup: Calories: 118, Total Protein: 2 gm., Soy Protein: 2 gm., Fat: 2 gm., Carbohydrates: 24 gm., Calcium: 16 mg., Fiber 1 gm., Sodium: 15 mg.

CHOCOLATE TAPIOCA: Along with the vanilla, add 6 oz. (½ cup) semisweet chocolate chips, and whip until they are melted and blended in.

Per ½ Cup: Calories: 154, Total Protein: 3 gm., Soy Protein: 2 gm., Fat: 3 gm., Carbohydrates: 24 gm., Calcium: 16 mg., Fiber 2 gm., Sodium: 16 mg.

TOFU CRÈME PARFAIT

This colorful, creamy dessert is featured on the cover.

For the Tofu Crème:
1-10.5 oz. pkg. silken tofu
⅓ cup sweetener of choice
1 Tbsp. unbleached flour
1 tsp. vanilla

For the Strawberry Filling:
½ lb. strawberries
¼ cup sweetener of choice
2 Tbsp. cornstarch

1. ***Tofu Crème:*** Blend the tofu, sweetener, and flour in a food processor or blender until smooth and creamy. ***Microwave Method:*** Cook 3 minutes on high, and whip. ***Stovetop Method:*** Cook over medium heat, stirring constantly until thickened. Pour the Tofu Crème evenly into 4 individual serving dishes.

2. ***Strawberry Filling:*** Blend the strawberries, sweetener, and cornstarch in a food processor or blender until smooth. ***Microwave Method:*** Cook on high for 2 minutes, whip, cook on high 2 more minutes, and whip. ***Stovetop Method:*** Cook over medium heat stirring constantly until thickened. Pour the Strawberry Filling evenly on top of the Tofu Crème. Chill until firm and serve topped with Creamy Tofu Topping (page 127)

Per Serving: Calories: 173, Total Protein: 6 gm., Soy Protein: 5 gm., Fat: 1 gm., Carbohydrates: 35 gm., Calcium: 10 mg., Fiber 1 gm., Sodium: 71 mg.

VARIATION: Substitute other berries or fruit in the Strawberry Filling. Try doubling the recipe to fill a baked Soy Cookie Pie Crust (page 139).

SOY COOKIE PIE CRUST

This makes a soft, cookie-like crust, especially good with fruit tarts or cream pies.

½ cup sugar
2 Tbsp. soy oil
½ tsp. vanilla
¼ cup water
2 Tbsp. soy powder
1¼ cups unbleached flour
1 tsp. baking powder

1. Preheat the oven to 350°F.

2. Mix the dry the ingredients in a food processor. While the processor is running, add the wet ingredients, and process only until mixed. Gather together and roll and shape in a pie pan. Prick and bake for 20 minutes or until browned.

Per Serving: Calories: 140, Total Protein: 3 gm., Soy Protein: 1 gm., Fat: 2 gm., Carbohydrates: 25 gm., Calcium: 32 mg., Fiber 1 gm., Sodium: 33 mg.

PUMPKIN SOY CUSTARD

Here is a creamy holiday pie without the cholesterol.

1-1 lb. can pumpkin
1 unbaked 9" pie shell
2 cups soy milk
1½ cups brown sugar
¼ cup sorghum or molasses
6 Tbsp. cornstarch
2 tsp. cinnamon
1 tsp. ginger
½ tsp. nutmeg
½ tsp. salt

1. Preheat the oven to 350°F.

2. Blend the rest of the ingredients together in a food processor or blender. Pour into an unbaked pie shell, and bake for about 1 hour or until set.

Per Serving: Calories: 310, Total Protein: 3 gm., Soy Protein: 2 gm., Fat: 8 gm., Carbohydrates: 54 gm., Calcium: 55 mg., Fiber 3 gm., Sodium: 303 mg.

BLACKBERRY SOY
FROGURT

YIELD: 5 CUPS

Always have your frogurt or ice cream mix as cold as possible before putting into the freezing machine. Freezing time will vary, but generally it takes about 6 to 7 minutes per quart.

3 cups soy yogurt
1½ cups blackberries
1 cup sweetener of choice
1 Tbsp. soy lecithin
⅛ tsp salt

1. Blend all the ingredients together in a blender until smooth and creamy, and freeze according to your ice cream machine instructions.

Per Cup: Calories: 238, Total Protein: 5 gm., Soy Protein: 4 gm., Fat: 5 gm., Carbohydrates: 43 gm., Calcium: 20 mg., Fiber 4 gm., Sodium: 73 mg.

MANGO SOY FROGURT

A cool, creamy, sweet mango treat.

3 cups soy yogurt
1½ cups mango, puréed
1 cup sweetener of choice, or to taste
1 Tbsp. soy lecithin

1. Blend all the ingredients together in a blender until smooth and creamy, and freeze according to your ice cream machine instructions.

Per Cup: Calories: 288, Total Protein: 4 gm., Soy Protein: 4 gm., Fat: 2 gm., Carbohydrates: 62 gm., Calcium: 14 mg., Fiber 3 gm., Sodium: 22 mg.

VANILLA SOY ICE

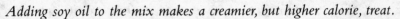

CREAM

YIELD: ABOUT 5 CUPS

Adding soy oil to the mix makes a creamier, but higher calorie, treat.

3 cups soy milk
1 cup sweetener of choice
¼ cup soy oil (opt.)
2 tsp. vanilla
pinch of salt
1 Tbsp. liquid soy lecithin

1. Blend all the ingredients together in a blender until smooth and creamy, and freeze according to your ice cream machine instructions.

Per Cup: Calories: 215, Total Protein: 4 gm., Soy Protein: 4 gm., Fat: 5 gm., Carbohydrates: 38 gm., Calcium: 6 mg., Fiber 2 gm., Sodium: 39 mg.

PEACHY SOY ICE CREAM

YIELD: ABOUT 6 CUPS

Try this at the height of peach season when the fruit is at its sweetest and most plentiful.

3 cups soy milk
1½ cups fresh or frozen peaches, sliced
1 cup sweetener of choice, or to taste
¼ cup soy oil (opt.)
1 Tbsp. soy lecithin
1 tsp. vanilla
⅛ tsp. salt

1. Blend all the ingredients together in a blender until smooth and creamy, and freeze according to your ice cream machine instructions. If you prefer chunks of peaches, chop the peaches separately, and fold into the soymilk mixture just before freezing.

Per Cup: Calories: 177, Total Protein: 5 gm., Soy Protein: 4 gm., Fat: 2 gm., Carbohydrates: 35 gm., Calcium: 9 mg., Fiber 3 gm., Sodium: 73 mg.

DRINKS &
YOGURT

SOY NOG

YIELD: 2 CUPS

Serve Soy Nog *for holiday cheer without the cholesterol.*

2 cups soymilk
¼ cup sweetener of choice
1 tsp. vanilla
¼ tsp. rum extract
pinch of nutmeg

Combine all the ingredients in a blender until smooth and frothy. Serve hot or cold.

Per Cup: Calories: 209, Total Protein: 7 gm., Soy Protein: 7 gm., Fat: 4 gm., Carbohydrates: 37 gm., Calcium: 12 mg., Fiber 3 gm., Sodium: 31 mg.

HOT SOY CHOCOLATE

YIELD: 2 CUPS

This can be served hot or cold.

2 cups soymilk
2 Tbsp. cocoa powder
4-5 Tbsp. sweetener of choice, or to taste

1. Combine all the ingredients in a blender until smooth and frothy.

Per Cup: Calories: 203, Total Protein: 8 gm., Soy Protein: 7 gm., Fat: 4 gm., Carbohydrates: 31 gm., Calcium: 18 mg., Fiber 5 gm., Sodium: 31 mg.

COCOA OR CAROB
BANANA SOY SHAKE

YIELD: 3 CUPS (2 SERVINGS)

This frothy shake makes a hearty snack.

1 cup soymilk
½ medium fresh or frozen banana
3 Tbsp. sweetener of choice, or to taste
1 Tbsp. cocoa or carob powder

1. Combine all the ingredients in a blender, and blend until smooth and frothy.

Per Serving: Calories: 337, Total Protein: 9 gm., Soy Protein: 7 gm., Fat: 5 gm., Carbohydrates: 63 gm., Calcium: 27 mg., Fiber 8 gm., Sodium: 34 mg.

CAFE AU LAIT DE SOYA

YIELD: 1 CUP

This is a light, non-cafeinated hot or cold drink.

1 cup soymilk
1-2 Tbsp. sweetener of choice, or to taste
4 tsp. grain beverage crystals, or to taste

1. Combine all the ingredients in a blender, and blend until smooth and frothy. Serve cold or heat and serve hot.

Per Cup: Calories: 147, Total Protein: 7 gm., Soy Protein: 7 gm., Fat: 4 gm., Carbohydrates: 21 gm., Calcium: 10 mg., Fiber 3 gm., Sodium: 29 mg.

SOY BERRY SMOOTHIE

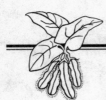

2 cups soymilk
1 cup blueberries, strawberries, raspberries, or blackberries,
    or ½ lb. frozen strawberries,
    or ¼ lb. frozen blueberries
¼ cup sweetener of choice, or to taste
1 tsp. vanilla

1. Combine all the ingredients in a blender, blend until smooth and frothy, and serve immediately.

Per Serving: Calories: 250, Total Protein: 7 gm., Soy Protein: 7 gm., Fat: 4 gm.,
Carbohydrates: 46 gm., Calcium: 17 mg., Fiber 5 gm., Sodium: 36 mg.

PEACH-BANANA SOY

SHAKE

Yield: 2 cups

1 cup soymilk
½ cup (¼ lb.) fresh or frozen peaches
½ medium fresh or frozen banana,
2 Tbsp. sweetener of choice, or to taste
½ tsp. vanilla

1. Combine all the ingredients in a blender, and blend until smooth and frothy.

Per Cup: Calories: 135, Total Protein: 4 gm., Soy Protein: 4 gm., Fat: 2 gm., Carbohydrates: 25 gm., Calcium: 10 mg., Fiber 3 gm., Sodium: 15 mg.

SOY YOGURT

YIELD: 1 GALLON

Soy Yogurt *is a creamy, tangy treat made by the same process as dairy yogurt. Making yogurt is a simple process, but it takes some time and preparation. I use glass pint or quart canning jars and their lids for containers and hot soymilk from our soy dairy. You can may make your own soymilk from beans, or use soymilk made from soymilk powder, or use asceptically packaged, unflavored soymilk. Soy yogurt will keep for up to two weeks in the refrigerator.*

1 gallon soymilk
glass canning jars and lids
a ladle or cup
stainless steel spoon
jar tongs
candy thermometer (opt.)
1 cup active or live yogurt or a yogurt culture

1. Begin by sterilizing the containers and equipment. Use a pot large enough to hold the jars, lids, ladle or cup (for dipping out the hot soymilk), spoon (for stirring the yogurt starter culture), tongs (for lifting out the hot jars), and thermometer. Cover and steam or boil everything for at least 20 minutes.

2. Heat the milk to boiling while stirring constantly. Remove the jars from the sterilizing pot with the sterilized tongs, setting them right side up on a towel. Pour or ladle the soymilk into the sterilized jars, leaving room to add 1 to 2 Tbsp. yogurt starter culture. Put the lids on loosely to cover the jars, but don't seal. Let the soymilk cool to 110°F, or until the jar feels warm to the inside of your wrist but does not burn. You can lift a lid and check the temperature with a sterilized thermometer.

3. Add 1 Tbsp. of any plain yogurt with a live culture to each pint of soymilk. Check the carton label to make sure the culture is live. If you would rather not use a dairy yogurt as a starter, there

are freeze dried vegan yogurt starters available at most health or natural food stores. Follow the package directions for the right amount to use. Briskly stir in the starter with the sterilized spoon, and cover tightly with the sterilized lid.

4. Place the jars in a heavy duty portable cooler or foam ice chest (without ice, of course) and close it up tightly. Let the yogurt incubate undisturbed for 2 to 6 hours until set. The yogurt is ready if it separates cleanly and easily from the sides of the jar when gently tilted. Refrigerate the finished yogurt. An alternative method for incubation is to have a heavy quilt laid out and folded in half with a towel in the center to protect it from any drips. Arrange the sealed jars in the center, then fold the quilt evenly over, using clothes pins to secure it. Still another method for incubation is to wrap the jars in an electric blanket set on a low setting.

Per Cup: Calories: 82, Total Protein: 7 gm., Soy Protein: 7 gm., Fat: 4 gm., Carbohydrates: 4 gm., Calcium: 17 mg., Fiber 3 gm., Sodium: 32 mg.

SOY YOGURT CHEESE

Yield 2 cups

This is a creamy, tangy cheese that can be used as you would cream cheese. Try it in Tofu Tiramisu *(page 124)*

1 quart Soy Yogurt (page 150)
coffee filter
strainer

1. Arrange a coffee filter in a strainer inside a bowl and pour the Soy Yogurt into the filter. Cover and let it stand to drain in the refrigerator until the liquid stops draining out (about 24 hours).

Per ¼ Cup: Calories: 40, Total Protein: 4 gm., Soy Protein: 4 gm., Fat: 2 gm., Carbohydrates: 2 gm., Calcium: 5 mg., Fiber 2 gm., Sodium: 15 mg.

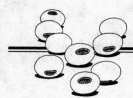

INDEX

Ask your store to carry these books, or you may
order directly from:

Book Publishing Company   **Or call: 1-800-695-2241**
P.O. Box 99   **Please add $2.50 per**
Summertown, TN 38483   **book for shipping**

Almost-No Fat Cookbook 12.95
Almost-No Fat Holiday Cookbook .12.95
Becoming Vegetarian 15.95
Burgers 'n Fries 'n Cinnamon Buns 6.95
Cookin' Healthy with One Foot Out the Door 8.95
Cooking with Gluten and Seitan 7.95
Delicious Jamaica 11.95
Ecological Cooking: Recipes to Save the Planet 10.95
Fabulous Beans 9.95
Foods that Cause You To Loose Weight 12.95
From the Global Kitchen 11.95
From A Traditional Greek Kitchen 11.95
Good Time Eatin' in Cajun Country 9.95
Indian Vegetarian Cooking at Your House 12.95
Instead of Chicken, Instead of Turkey 9.95
Kids Can Cook 9.95
Lighten Up with Louise Hagler 11.95
New Farm Vegetarian Cookbook 8.95
Now & Zen Epicure 17.95
Olive Oil Cookery 10.95
Peaceful Cook 8.95
Physician's Slimming Guide 5.95
Shiitake Way 7.95
Shoshoni Cookbook 12.95
Solar Cooking 8.95
The Sprout Garden 8.95
Table for Two 12.95
Tempeh Cookbook 10.95
Tofu Cookery 15.95
Tofu Quick and Easy 7.95
TVP® Cookbook 6.95
The Uncheese Cookbook 11.95
Uprisings: The Whole Grain Bakers' Book 13.95
Vegetarian Cooking for People with Diabetes 10.95
The Vegetarian Diet: A Dietitian's Guide to Sensible Eating . .14.95